To Really Love a Man

Praise for *To Really Love a Man*

"Read this book if you want to have a more loving, intimate, understanding and vulnerable relationship with the special person in your life." –John Gray, PhD, author of *Men are from Mars, Women are from Venus*.

"To say that Barry and Joyce Vissell are masters of love is not an exaggeration. Not only is their own marriage a model of the kind of relationship most of us would like to have, but they teach us what real, lasting love is all about. I highly recommend these two new books, and all their books and retreats to anyone who wants to have an enlightened relationship that lasts through time." –Jed Diamond, PhD, author of *The Enlightened Marriage*

"Barry and Joyce Vissell are two of the most sincere and compelling voices for healing relationships and creating the highest connections. They have devoted their lives to understanding and explaining what makes relationships work. The wisdom they share in these new books will absolutely help you create the kind of relationships your heart desires and you deserve." –Alan Cohen, author of *Don't Get Lucky, Get Smart*

"*To Really Love a Woman* and *To Really Love a Man* are backed by the powerful work the Vissells have been doing decade after decade in helping couples thrive and see the highest in one another, fueled by the beauty and success of their own partnership." –David Feinstein and Donna Eden, authors of *The Energies of Love*

"Joyce and Barry Vissell walk their talk. Having been together for 52 years and taught thousands of people how to love themselves and their partners, I am thrilled that they have shared their wisdom in these books. Their writing is a true representation of who they are: warm, caring, supportive, funny, and inspiring. Give yourself the gift of these books and watch all of your relationships transform!" –Karen Drucker, singer, songwriter, and author of *"Let Go of the Shore"*

"It's so easy to fall into tried-and-true patterns of showing love. The Vissells challenge us to let our imagination be big and to reach down deep to expand our repertoire of ways we show love. It's a detailed, practical, and inspirational guide for those who aspire to become great lovers and to bring maximum delight to their partnership." –Linda Bloom, co-author of *Secrets of Great Marriages*.

"Reading these two books is a blessing and transmission of decades of personal and couples work. These books are filled with teachings. Joyce and Barry have put truths into words that we were unable to articulate. We want to thank them from our hearts for creating an authentic map that we can trust and feel confident to follow." –Barbara and Mark Stefik, authors of *The Zorcon World Stories*

To Really Love a Man

by Joyce Vissell, RN, MS & Barry Vissell, MD

authors of The Shared Heart, Models of Love, Risk To Be Healed, The Heart's Wisdom, Meant To Be, and A Mother's Final Gift

To Really Love a Man

Copyright © 2018 by Ramira Publishing
PO Box 2140, Aptos, CA 95001-2140. 831.684.2299.
www.SharedHeart.org.

All rights reserved. No part of this book may be used or reproduced in any manner whatsoever without written permission, except in the case of brief quotations in articles or reviews.

ISBN-13: 978-0-9612720-8-1
Library of Congress Control Number: 2017942524

Printed in the United States of America on acid-free, chlorine-free, and Sustainable Forestry Initiative (SFI) certified paper.

Cover design by Melinda Lawton.
Cover photo by Barry Vissell

Also by Barry and Joyce Vissell:

The Shared Heart: Relationship Initiations and Celebrations
Models of Love: The Parent-Child Journey
Risk to be Healed: The Heart of Personal and Relationship Growth
Light in the Mirror: A New Way to Understand Relationships
Meant To Be: Miraculous True Stories to Inspire a Lifetime of Love
A Mother's Final Gift: How One Woman's Courageous Dying Transformed her Family
And by Rami Vissell:
Rami's Book: The Inner Life of a Child

Acknowledgements

We are grateful to our editing angels, John Drew, Nancy Collins, Elisabeth Hallett, Meg Rinaldi, Jackson Roesch, Lisa Kingsbury, Liliana Cartagena, Pam Schott, and Dawn Song.

Thank you Melinda Lawton for the beautiful book cover.

Thanks to all the couples who contributed their words of wisdom, and to the couples who became examples in these pages.

And always our thanks to the One who continually teaches us to really love.

For our parents:

Louise and Hank Wollenberg and
Helen and Michael Vissell
Always loving us from beyond

our children:

Rami, Mira, and John-Nuriel
How proud we are of all three of you

and our grandchildren:

Skye and Owen
Keeping our hearts wide open

To Really Love a Man

Contents

Introduction 1
   The Platinum Rule of Relationship 3
To Really Appreciate a Man...................................6
   The Super Appreciator 6
   Find Out What He Needs..................................10
   How have I needed to be appreciated by Joyce?............13
   Exercising the Appreciation Muscle 17
You Said "No" and Changed My Life 21
To Really Choose a Man 24
To Really Trust a Man...31
   First you must trust yourself. 31
   Trust him by being vulnerable with him.......34
   Trust Practice 37
To Really Love the Little Boy Inside the Man....38
   The Hidden Inner Child 39
   How Joyce Loves my Inner Little Boy 44
   Inner Practice 47
   Relationship Practice......................................48
To Really Make Love to a Man 49
   Sexual Moments..58
   Sexual Communication: What You Appreciate 62
   Sexual Communication: What You Need......64
   Loving a Man by Taking Care of Your Body 65
   Challenges to Sexually Loving a Man...........68

- *The Two Sides of Impotence* 70
- *Menopause* 73
- Helping a Man to Play 74
- To Really Love a Man is to Love His Family 79
  - *Feelings and Boundaries* 82
  - *Some tips for connecting with your man's parents* 87
  - *More on Boundaries* 89
  - *Remember to be thoughtful of his parents* 90
- Love Him in Public Too 92
- To Really Become Vulnerable with a Man 96
  - *Vulnerability-Challenged* 97
  - *Practice* 102
- To Really Love the Father in a Man 106
- To Really Receive a Man 110
  - *Practice* 117
- To Really Listen to a Man 118
  - *Twenty-Minute Listening Exercise* 123
- Using Our Words Wisely 128
- Find Out What He Really Wants and Needs 132
  - *Sharing His Vision* 135
  - *Getting Your Man Out in Nature* 137
  - *Going on Adventures with Barry* 142
- Apologizing to a Man 147
  - *Taking Responsibility* 153
- To Resolve Conflict with a Man 157
  - *Irritation vs Anger* 158
  - *Beneath Anger* 163
  - *To Effectively Argue with a Man* 166

 Specific Rules for Effectively Arguing with a Man....170
 Resolving Arguments...172
 Don't Wait Until It's Too Late...................................175
 Remembering the Love and Letting the Rest Go........179
Money and Loving a Man..183
To Really Accept Who He Is...194
 Inner Practice 198
You Love Him by Knowing You Are Equals....................199
To Really Love the Man Within...204
 Positive Projections Can Also Hurt............................205
 Practice: Loving your Inner Man................................208
To Know the God in Your Man 210
 Inner Practice: Communing with His God Self.........217
 Outer Practice: Seeing His God Self 218

"When your innermost tender feelings can be spoken without fear or shame…

When you can see your divine goddess-self reflected in his eyes…

When you feel most beautiful in his presence…

You know you really love a man."

– Barry Vissell

Introduction

HOW DOES A MAN REALLY NEED TO BE LOVED? How can his partner help to bring out his sensitivity, his emotions, his strength, his fire, and at the same time allow him to feel respected, secure, and acknowledged?

We feel that women and men are essentially similar souls in different-sexed bodies. Both sexes want the same happiness, need the same love, crave the same peace, and feel the same emotions. In all our previous books we have emphasized the similarity rather than the difference between the sexes. While this is the highest truth, there is another truth no less important. Most men and women approach life and relationship in different ways and react to situations differently. Notice we said "most," because nothing is all or none. However, the difference in male and female hormones, the findings of brain chemistry research, added to the difference in how women and men are raised, help create different emotional climates and even alter ways of thinking. On the deepest level, women and men are alike. In personality, there is often a clear contrast. On the level of soul there is sameness. In thoughts and feelings, men and women can be strikingly different.

We write these books not to point out the differences between the sexes. There are enough books that do that. We write these books to give tools to the readers to more deeply honor their partners. With honoring there can be joining. Respect for differences breaks down the age-old wall between women and men. Before there can be union, there must be love. Before there can be love, there must be understanding and respect. Before there can be understanding and respect, there must be listening -- real listening – both inner and outer.

To really love another is to more deeply love yourself. To more deeply understand another is to more deeply understand your own soul. In other words, the real opportunity of relationship is your own spiritual growth. As souls, we are both male and female. It is just in our bodies, minds, and emotions that we express one sex predominantly.

Although these writings refer mostly to heterosexual women and men, there is a wealth of information for LGBTQ. Our focus, after all, is how to deeply love another person, whether it be a man or a woman.

The Platinum Rule of Relationship

There's a new rule that's specific for intimate relationships. Most of us know the Golden Rule: Do unto others as you would have them do unto you. It works fine in many circumstances. If you're tempted to yell at the guy who just cut you off in traffic, you take a deep breath and give him the benefit of the doubt. After all, that could be you someday. You follow the Golden Rule when you visit a friend who's sick, because you would want the same treatment if you become sick.

The problem is, however, that the Golden Rule often does not work with intimate relationships, especially when it gets down to specific actions. For example, your partner may be content with the needle on the gas gauge hovering just above empty. If the car runs out of gas, it'll just be an annoying inconvenience. You, however, may be terrified at the proposition of running out of gas. It may bring up images of being stranded on the side of a road, and vulnerable to anyone with less than honorable motives.

Then there's the guy who goes to Home Depot to shop for a wedding anniversary present. If he could choose a gift for his wife to get him, it would be a new cordless drill and driver. So that's what he decides to get his wife. When she opens the gift on their anniversary, he's stymied by her lack of enthusiasm. He is, after all, following the Golden Rule.

There's a better rule for romantic relationships that bumps consciousness up to a higher level – The Platinum Rule – Do unto others as *they* would have you do unto *them*. In other words, treat others the way they want to be treated, rather than the way you want to be treated. It means you actually have to find out what he wants.

The Platinum Rule can actually be hard to follow. I have to get personal here. I love touch. Any touch is wonderful to me. I love it when Joyce takes my hand. I love it when she hugs me or even when she jumps on top of me when we're lying together. Now Joyce loves touch as well, but she also loves spoken words. They can be words of love or appreciation. They can be questions inviting her to share what she feels.

It's easy for me to slip into the Golden Rule with regard to touch and words. I can forget about her love of words and, instead, touch her because that's what I love. And don't get me wrong ... she appreciates this show of love through touch, even if it's not the only thing she wants. It's just that I need to remember the Platinum Rule, and switch to give Joyce both the touch and the words she wants. This shows my full love to her.

Is something wrong because you may have to ask him what he really wants, likes, or needs? Does that mean you're not the divine lover you want to be? It's lovely to try to guess these things and, sometimes by trial and error, you'll actually get it right. But we can't be mind readers all the time. If you want to be a divine lover, ask him often about his preferences. Remember, his preferences can change over time. Ask about mundane things, like food, clothing, types of exercise, books, or anything else. Also ask about important things, like what are his current dreams and goals for his life.

It's even good to gently remind him about what you really need and want. This is different from nagging, complaining, or controlling him. That's a turn-off for anyone. Instead, try inviting him to love you in a different way. Let's revisit Joyce's and my touch/talk preferences, but much more personally. During lovemaking, I may get a little too absorbed in the sensory experience, and become quiet. Joyce has a sweet way of saying, "Barry, I would love to hear your words right now." I hear this as an invitation to love her even more, rather than a put-down, or that I'm doing something wrong. My then opening to a flow of poetry, or even singing a love song to her, enhances not only her experience, but mine as well.

Want to be a better lover? Follow the Platinum Rule of relationship.

By the way, they do sell flowers at Home Depot.

To Really Appreciate a Man

WOMEN AND MEN BOTH NEED APPRECIATION. By this, we do not mean only compliments. Real appreciation is a gift of love straight from the heart, an acknowledgement of another's greatness, and a way of showing your partner that you really care.

Many men need specific kinds of appreciation. And you as a woman need to find out by asking him. Here's an example:

The Super Appreciator

Joanna fancied herself a great appreciator. She knew the importance of positive words and made it a point to appreciate Thomas as much as she could. In a couple's session with the two of them, Joanna pointed out the beauty of his soul, his caring and generosity, how loved she felt by him, even how attractive he was to her. Thomas, when it was his turn, appreciated how hard Joanna works taking care of the children and doing the absolute best for them.

We noticed, however, that Thomas looked sad, and pointed this out to him. He said Joanna's appreciations were so much more important than his. She pointed out the depths of his soul, and he could only acknowledge what she did. He wondered what was wrong with him. Yet he loved Joanna, and was committed to improving their relationship.

"Thomas," we asked, "is there some way you need to be appreciated that Joanna is missing?"

After a moment's hesitation he spoke, "This sounds petty, but Joanna seldom appreciates what I do. She focuses on the more important things, the spiritual things."

"Thomas," we interrupted, "you have a right to be appreciated and recognized for what you do. Your accomplishments are part of your beauty. Tell us the things you do well, the things you do for Joanna and for yourself."

"Well… I work hard at my job. I make the money, so Joanna can be with the kids at home. Then, when I'm home, I take care of the house, fixing, cleaning, and stuff. Joanna mentioned one time that the old birdfeeder was broken, so I went out to the garage and spent about an hour fixing it. I filled it with bird seed, hung it up, and it's been over a week. She hasn't said a thing. But I understand. She's busy with the kids and probably hasn't noticed it yet."

We stopped him again. "Thomas, you deserve to be appreciated for fixing that birdfeeder."

Joanna reached over and took Thomas's hand. She looked like she was about to cry, "I'm so sorry. I did notice the birdfeeder, but it didn't even occur to me to appreciate you for that. I didn't know it was important to you."

At that, Thomas's eyes welled up with tears. "My parents never appreciated me either for the things I did. Once,

I got the highest grade in the class, a B, and my mother criticized me for not getting an A. Or the first time my dad allowed me to mow the lawn, he criticized me for missing a few areas. It seemed like nothing I did was good enough."

We held his hands and spoke softly, "Thomas, there's a little boy inside you who still craves acknowledgement for the things he accomplishes."

We glanced at Joanna and gave her a nod urging her to speak to Thomas. Through her own tears she spoke, "I guess I'm not the great appreciator I thought I was. I didn't even know what my own husband needs the most. If I were your parent, I would be so proud of you for that B, for mowing that lawn, and for all the things you do in your life. By the way, the birdfeeder is beautiful…"

Thomas put up his hand to stop her and said, "You don't need to do this…"

But Joanna interrupted, "Please, let me. The birdfeeder IS beautiful. You did a great job fixing it. You can't even tell it was broken. I'm so sorry I haven't appreciated you the way you need. You work really hard so that we can live comfortably. And you never complain. I find that incredible. I vow to you right now to make it a point every day to appreciate what you do for us."

Thomas leaned toward Joanna and they hugged.

> *I so appreciate my husband's love expressed in everyday ways. I see his love in the way he shows up on time at the airport when my son and I have been away. He doesn't complain that we've gone on a trip without him; he just arrives at exactly the right time to bring us home, having parked the car and come into the airport, waiting at the foot of the escalator so that Zachary sees his daddy right away. I see his love in the way he reminds me to stop working and get to bed at a reasonable time most every night. I see his love in the way he drives my elderly mother to a meeting so that I can stay home and put Zachary to bed. I see his love in the quiet ways, for he is not a man who likes to speak of love. He just lives his love. Oh, we have our tussles. We argue over silly things; we try to change things we don't like in the other, but I am a better person for being in a relationship with this man, my husband.*
> –Ellen M. Wilson, El Paso, TX

Remember, this doesn't mean that all men need to be appreciated mainly for what they do. Just find out what kind of acknowledgment means most to the man in your life. Another example:

Find Out What He Needs

In a counseling session, we asked Olivia if she knew how Jacob most needed to be appreciated. She guessed, "Probably for the things he does for me." We looked over at Jacob, who had a pained expression on his face.

"She guessed wrong, didn't she?" we surmised.

Struggling for words, Jacob finally managed a yes.

Olivia looked at Jacob, "Then is it for what a good person you are?"

This time, still struggling with his feelings, he just shook his head from side to side.

"Then what is it that you need," she said with just a hint of exasperation.

Jacob looked at us, as if for encouragement.

I said, "Obviously, there's something you need that you're not getting. Tell her what it is."

Jacob's face flushed. He seemed embarrassed.

"This is not easy," he began. He forced himself to look at Olivia, but he looked like he wanted to run away. "I need you to appreciate me as a lover."

"But I do," she interrupted, "I feel loved by you. You're kind and thoughtful."

"That's not what I mean," he said with that same pained expression. "I need to be appreciated as a *sexual* lover, for how I am in the bedroom."

Olivia looked surprised. "I didn't know that's what you needed. I thought it was obvious that our lovemaking is special to me. I didn't know you needed reassurance."

"I guess I do," Jacob answered. "I'm sorry I've been too uncomfortable to ask for it."

"Well, I'm sorry I haven't come right out and said what a good lover you are. It's a little embarrassing that we're not alone," she said, glancing our way, "but let me say some things right now. I feel safe in your arms when we're making love. I feel special to you. You touch me in just the right ways." She paused a moment, then added, "Actually, I've never felt as satisfied with anyone else."

Jacob suddenly put his head in his hands and started sobbing, much to our surprise. Olivia took one of his hands and gently kissed it. He opened his eyes to meet hers, then said, "Once, early in our relationship, you told me about your first boyfriend when you were seventeen and how 'magical' sex was with him. Something about the way you said it, and then not saying anything about sex with me, I've been feeling insecure as a lover, that maybe you're not as happy with me as you were with him."

Jacob looked about as vulnerable as a person could get, baring his soul wide open. His lips were trembling and his eyes were moist with tears.

Olivia pulled him close in a tender embrace, and spoke softly, "Yes, Carl was my first lover, my first boyfriend, my first everything. That's why it was magical. But he could never commit to me. I would always catch him flirting with other girls. I never felt completely safe in his arms, like I do with you. Feeling your deep commitment to our marriage has made sex a thousand times more magical than it was with Carl."

Jacob's face was now lit up with joy.

It was time for us to speak. "Jacob, do you see how important it was for you to bring this out into the open? Yes, it took courage and vulnerability, but look at the result. A whole piece of insecurity was based upon a made-up story, and not fact. And Olivia, now you know the appreciation Jacob most needs, at least for now."

How does he most need to be appreciated? You may be surprised. Then make it a practice as much as you can to offer this specific appreciation.

Please don't get the idea that men don't also need appreciation for inner qualities of being. We have met many couples where the man was appreciated for what he did *and* as a lover, but he really needed to be seen and acknowledged on the level of his soul, for qualities like compassion, generosity, integrity or trustworthiness. He needed to be appreciated for who he is, more than what he does.

How have I needed to be appreciated by Joyce?

It has changed over the years as I, and my needs and insecurities, have changed. In *To Really Love a Woman*, I shared a story of the first time I was truly vulnerable with Joyce. We were just married, and I felt insecure and scared to go back to a very difficult situation in medical school. Showing Joyce all my vulnerability also showed her how much I needed her. It opened, for her, a window into my soul, and she poured out the fullness of her heart's love, filling me through that window. She deeply appreciated my inner beauty and greatness.

Did I know I needed appreciation for my inner beauty and greatness? No, not consciously at least. It certainly wasn't something I could have ever asked for, but this was indeed my greatest need at the time.

> *I feel so loved by Fran when I share with her my deepest fear and pain and she looks at me with shining eyes and says only, "I understand."*
> – Gary, Malibu, VA

As a young father, I had my share of insecurity. I sometimes had difficulty with my boundaries between work and family. I see now that the extra hours at work were not the healthiest choice, and robbed me of time I could've been with the children. Some evenings I came home after the children were asleep, completely missing out on the delightful bedtime rituals, the stories, the songs and prayers. Sometimes I felt the children needed Joyce more than me (my rationalization), so I just let her do more of the parenting. But inside, I sometimes felt inadequate as a father, ill-equipped to really love and nurture my children.

What helped me most was Joyce's appreciation of me as a father. No, she wasn't perfect. Sometimes she would complain that I wasn't there enough, but the appreciation was always deeper. She would say things like, "Barry, you are such a loving father. You know exactly what each child needs. They light up when you come into the room. You make up the best games of anyone I know." And just as important, "You're also a loving father to the little girl inside me." These appreciations touched and helped to heal that place of insecurity in me. They inspired me to become more of what Joyce was seeing and appreciating.

> *Barry, when you give your love to our children, you give your love to me at the same time. I know sometimes you're busy with so much pressure in the office, and our son walks in needing your help with his homework. I see you take a deep breath, let go of everything you're doing, give it all up just to be there for our son.*

And now we also have our first grandson, Skye. Here's what Joyce writes:

> *Barry, I love watching you with Skye. I am amazed at your ability to make up games using whatever is in front of you. The large green pillows in the living room instantly become the building blocks of an elaborate house or fort. His toy trucks carry unimaginable objects to equally unimaginable places. And even if you have nothing to play with, your hand becomes transformed into a person who can walk, dance, and jump onto Skye's head, making him laugh with delight.*

Then there were the times I stopped taking care of myself spiritually, like meditating, or giving myself quiet time for soul reflection. I judged myself less spiritual than Joyce. Joyce read spiritual books. I didn't. When Joyce appreciated my deep spiritual nature, it always felt so reaffirming.

There were also times over the years when I felt less secure about our sexual connection or my own sexuality. I remember one time after sex when I judged my performance, and Joyce's appreciation helped me so much by widening my focus from one little detail that didn't work to the bigger picture of sexuality where the real ecstasy is the union of minds, hearts, feelings and souls, as well as bodies.

As you can see, sometimes your man knows how he needs to be appreciated, and sometimes not. So you can't sit back and wait to be invited by him, nor does it always work to ask him what he needs, or give the appreciation that you most need (the Golden Rule). The key is to get out of yourself enough to feel what he needs, and then dare to give that appreciation. If he lights up, you've hit the right spot. If he has no reaction, you still may have hit the right spot. As we say in our third book, *Risk To Be Healed*, "You can never judge the effect of your love and appreciation by your partner's response." If he reacts to what you have said with a look of sadness, upset, pain, or any other negative expression, you may or may not have hit the right spot, but it may be time to back off and give him a little room. First offer comfort, then give him room. Remember, this is not about you. Loving someone through appreciation is one of the highest art forms. It takes a huge risk, but it's worth everything.

> *I feel most loved by Ruth when she tells me how proud she is of my ability to grow and change.*
> –Bruce Richardson, South Royalton, VT

Exercising the Appreciation Muscle

Joyce: I love to appreciate Barry and have always enjoyed this. When we were first married, I would appreciate him and there would be nothing coming back in return. He would smile at me, but remain silent. I realized that Barry's lack of verbal appreciation of me was not because he did not love me, because I knew he did, and he showed me in abundance with his non-verbal affection and caring. Spoken appreciation was just not something his family did, so he hadn't developed the skill.

I decided that I would keep on appreciating him and perhaps, in time, he would feel how good it felt and return the appreciations. This may sound strange, but I was all right with this. It took four years for this pattern to change. Remember, we were also very young and he was in a challenging medical school program at USC, so there was not a lot of time to practice.

After four years he started appreciating me, minimally at first and the appreciations were not that deep. It was like developing a new muscle in which the strength came slowly. But once that muscle was finally developed, he exercised it to the max. I would say that now he appreciates me as much if not more than I do him, and his appreciations are very deep. It took determination on my part to not give up, and just keep appreciating him. It has been well worth it, for my life is filled with appreciation from him now.

Barry loves when I appreciate his sexuality. I tell him on a regular basis that, if all men could learn from him about how to please a woman sexually, this world would be a better place. I feel that he is the most wonderful lover and I want him to know that, so I take every opportunity I can to tell him.

I also appreciate him for his spirituality and this is important for him to hear. I appreciate him for being my best friend and for bringing so much laughter, adventure and fun into my life. I appreciate him for being so wise and being such a good partner in our work together.

But the very hardest appreciations, and perhaps the most important, are when I am not feeling so much love for him because we are not getting along. At these times, which occurred more often when we were younger, it feels as if the darkness is closing in around us. During these dark times, the appreciation is most important as it helps to bring back the light.

This always reminds me of our wedding. Barry and I were married on the coldest, darkest night of the year. December 21, 1968 had subzero weather with a blinding snowstorm. We said our vows on that solstice eve in a darkened church with only the light of two candles held between us. Though it was dark, the light of just these two small candles gave warmth, hope and radiance to our spoken words.

After the ceremony, many said it was the most beautiful wedding they had witnessed. "The light was so bright," they remarked with enthusiasm. How could two small candles create so much light? We were only twenty-two years old and rather naive. We didn't know about the symbolism of the darkness and light at the time of the winter solstice. We picked that time because Barry was free from medical school. We picked the dark evening of the solstice because it was the only time the church was available.

Yet, over the years, I have often reflected on how perfect it was for us to be married in the dark coldness of winter. There have been many times in our marriage when the darkness seemed to be crowding in, almost suffocating our love. There were times when the cold darkness between us made us feel we didn't want to try anymore. It was during these dark times in our marriage that we would remember the blinding snowstorm on the black night of our wedding, and how two small candles had brought so much warmth and radiance. The light of these candles represented our simple love and appreciation of each other.

So, surrounded by the darkness of our minds and emotions, we would once again speak simple words of appreciation to each other. The powerful act of appreciation fanned the smoldering embers in our covered-over hearts, which then glowed brighter as more and more kind words were spoken. Soon there was enough of a flame and warm radiance to allow for the deeper expressions of love.

The darkness was still all around us. It hadn't gone away, just like the darkness outside the church so many years ago. Yet the candlelight of our open hearts gave vision, hope, understanding and a safe haven from the shadow areas of our relationship. Simple words of appreciation and love can light the way in relationship and are a beautiful way to love a man.

You Said "No" and Changed My Life

A POWERFUL WAY I HAVE FELT THE MOST LOVED BY YOU, my beloved Joyce, started many years ago with your saying no to me. Not saying no to who I am or to my love, but saying no to who I'm not. You learned to say no to my pressuring you to do things that you didn't feel right doing. You were able to say the big no to my sexual fling with your friend – you left the relationship. That leaving – that saying no – allowed me to respect you so much more. When you left that night, you said in your note, "Our relationship is over. You crossed too big a line this time. I will always love you, but I can no longer live with you as wife and husband. So now I give you your freedom to live as you wish, to do whatever you want, whenever you want it."

Your love for me in that message was plain to see. At the time, of course, it was sheer agony. I didn't want you to leave. I wanted you to stay, but I wasn't willing to respect your feelings. Now I see how your no was an enormous yes. You were saying yes to my deepest growth as a human and spiritual being. You were saying yes to our future children and grandchildren, to our work and service in the world, to my heart of hearts. That no made it possible for me to start my real work of loving myself, rather than looking for love only on the outside. And my working on truly loving myself allowed us to continue our marriage, rather than end it.

Your learning to clearly say no allowed you to say many more yeses to me. Respecting your own boundary was a profound gift of love to me, and it allowed you to say yes to things that sometimes were not comfortable for you, but gave you opportunities to grow. You could then say yes to my vision of our work together, which has now become your vision as well.

When you learned to say no to me, you learned to say yes to yourself. Your focus shifted from loving only me to loving yourself as well. Before my affair, I was preoccupied with my needs, and you were focused on loving me. After my affair, we both learned to love you more, bringing sweet balance back to our relationship.

While walking on the beach the other day, you shared with me an image that you had been reflecting about. You described the container of your life with different-sized stones. The largest stone represented your relationship with yourself – your own heart and God. The next biggest stone represented me. Then smaller stones tapering down in size, symbolized our children, your service and purpose in the world. Then the stones got smaller and smaller until there was only sand filling the rest of the container of your life. I told you about the little pang of disappointment about my being a "next biggest stone." That disappointment came from my ego, the part of me that wants to be the most important "stone" in your life. In my heart, I am forever grateful that I am not the most important thing in your life. I love being the next biggest stone.

Do you see? Truly loving yourself has been the way you have loved me the most. All you now do to awaken more love in your heart also overflows that love to me. When you take the time to go to your little sanctuary in the woods to pray, to meditate, to do Tai Chi, to read inspiring words, to feel your feelings and your heart, you love me the best. When we then meet on the trail or back in the house, you greet me as a long-lost lover. When you make "love" more important than your beloved, your beloved feels more loved. Your honoring of your spirituality allows me to feel the most honored by you. Your commitment to the largest stone, to the highest within you, is the greatest gift you have ever given to me.

To Really Choose a Man

TO REALLY LOVE A MAN IS TO CHOOSE HIM OVER AND OVER AGAIN. It's not enough to say marriage vows one time, though that is certainly important. The relationship is deepened if you let him know often that you would choose him all over again if given the choice.

On the morning of our daughter's afternoon wedding, a friend came to set up the sound system. I was outside preparing flowers around the altar when he handed the microphone to me and said, "Say the most important thing in your heart right now."

I didn't even need to think about it when I clearly and with conviction said, "BARRY, WHEREVER YOU ARE, I CHOOSE YOU ALL OVER AGAIN. I WOULD MARRY YOU AGAIN IN A SECOND!"

From down at the bottom of our sixteen acres, Barry was clearing poison oak and yelled up, "JOYCE, I WILL ALWAYS CHOOSE YOU!"

I'm quite sure all of our neighbors heard our booming testimony of love and choosing, which I thought was sweet.

There are many things that stand in the way of a woman clearly choosing her partner as the most important person in her life. For many women, their children become more important than the man in their life, even if that man happens to be the father of the children. Having raised three children, I certainly understand this pull to make the children more important. I was a hands-on stay-at-home mother. I was and still am so in love with our children. When our first child, Rami, was born, I thought she was the cutest thing in the whole world. If I was in a room and she walked in after being away for a while with Barry, I would make such a big fuss over her and go on and on about how cute she was.

If Barry walked in right after her, I would look at him and think to myself, "What could he do right now to help me." He was becoming more of my helper than my partner. All of my adoration was going to Rami. One day Barry sat down next to me and said in a vulnerable voice, "I wish you could be as enthusiastic when I enter the room as you are with Rami."

He was absolutely right. I was giving a clear message that I was choosing Rami over him. I vowed to stop that right away. From then on, I sincerely tried to be enthusiastic about both of them. I vowed to stop seeing Barry simply as someone who could help me with the children, and see him as my partner, the man that I love and adore. From that time on, I made a point to let him know I would choose him again if given the choice. I also tell him I feel I made the best choice in a husband.

A woman's friends can also stand in the way of her choosing her husband or partner. I know women who would much rather spend time with their women friends than their partners. As a woman, I know how vitally important it is to have women friends. I know that most women feel they could not even survive this life without their women friends or, in some cases, their sisters. There are so many gifts that come from having women friends, like receiving their understanding of your feelings, body changes, mothering issues, or just the special bonding that can happen between women. However, some women do this to excess in which they are clearly choosing their women friends over the man in their life. The man is relegated to the background. He becomes a convenient person to watch the children, earn money, or help with the house. If the man feels second to the women friends, he will then go off and develop his own interests, and soon the two are merely passing each other as strangers in their home. This cycle will get worse unless there is a renewed choosing of each other.

Interestingly, body image can also become more important to a woman than the man she loves. Of course, exercise and working out is important in a woman's life, but not more than choosing love. She can become too preoccupied with how she looks. Hour upon hour can be spent in the gym sculpting a certain look to her body.

Then there's the food. The man returns from a hard day at work, possibly even physical work, to find a salad with non-calorie dressing waiting for him. What he wants and needs is a more substantial meal but is told that it is too tempting to eat that kind of fattening food. The man starts eating out with his friends and starts to feel that the way her body looks is more important than him.

I know a couple who were deeply in love and, before they got married, the man told her that his greatest dream was to have children with her. She agreed and made it part of their marriage vows to have a family together. The woman, who had been slightly overweight for her small frame, started working out and running. She devoted anywhere from five to six hours a day to creating the "perfect" body.

They had been together for several years when the man wanted to start having their family. For two years they tried every month, but she never got pregnant. They went to a fertility expert who simply stated that she was working out too much. Her body needed to become more open to a pregnancy, and the extreme workouts were blocking the hormones necessary for pregnancy. He suggested she experiment and cut down her rigorous workout time by half. She left that office and told her husband she would not even consider cutting out any of her workout. He told her that the way her body looked was not important to him. He just loved her for who she was, not for how she looked. She stubbornly asserted she would never give up any of her workout time.

He was deeply saddened as he knew then that his dream of having children with her might never be met. She was clearly choosing her body image. They tried for several more years but she never got pregnant. To cope with the disappointment, she added more hours to her routine. When the husband could no longer tolerate his feelings of abandonment, he left the marriage.

Sometimes women choose their family of origin over their partner. Their siblings and parents become more important than the men in their lives. I know several men who have to spend every single holiday and vacation with the women's family. One man lamented that he thought he was marrying one woman when instead he married her whole family of fifteen members. Every Christmas, Thanksgiving, Easter and each and every vacation he had from work was spent with her family. It was hard to feel the togetherness in their relationship around so many people. When he once asked if they could just spend one vacation totally alone, not only did she refuse, but he also then had her whole family upset with him for even coming up with the suggestion. This man loved his wife very much and did not want to leave her, but he always felt secondary to her family.

Career is another factor that can prevent a woman from really choosing her man. She and her partner may have come to agreements on childcare and hours of work. And yet, because it is harder for a woman in the professional workforce to prove herself, she may feel driven to spend many extra hours at night preparing for the next day. Doing well in her career may be her top priority and her partner may find himself further and further down her list.

Even spirituality can get in the way of a woman choosing her man. I consider spirituality very important, really the most important thing in life. And yet, even in this area, women can sometimes make unhealthy choices. When I was a young teenager my mother, who was a spiritual person, made a subtle choice of her church over my father. My brother had left for college and so that meant there were just three of us at home. My mother and father had some marriage problems that they were not addressing. I do not know what they were, but I could feel the tension. Instead of working out these problems, my mother started spending more and more of her time at the church. She was on every committee imaginable.

When my father came home from work, she would have dinner waiting for him and would have left early for an "important" church meeting. My father and I spent every evening alone for what seemed to me like a full year. He would help me with my homework, so it was a bonding time for us, but we both missed my mother. Even on Saturdays, she would work at the church as a volunteer. Sundays, we would go to church, and then my mother would invite college students over for a good home-cooked meal for lunch. My father and I did all of the dishes in the kitchen while my mother talked with them over coffee in the dining room.

For that year, I never saw my mother spend any time with my father. Something must have happened, because she gradually stopped being on so many committees, and returned to being a wife and mother. We had family meals, and my parents became a happy couple once again. My mother's relationship with God was still extremely important to her, but she chose to also give enough attention to my father.

My parents went on to have sixty memorable years together. Toward the end of his life, my father lost his hearing completely and no longer wanted to go to church. My mother would go alone and then quickly come home again and take him out to his favorite restaurant for lunch. She refused all of the many invitations to go out to lunch with her friends and instead chose my father.

In our counseling practice, we sometimes will ask a couple if they would choose each other again. I will never forget the look on one man's face when his wife, without any doubt in her voice, said she would choose him again and again. The man burst into tears. He had been convinced that she was merely tolerating the relationship. His heart opened wide just knowing that she would choose him again.

To Really Trust a Man

Joyce and I listened to the pain of a woman who spoke about her two failed marriages, and the abuse she experienced in each. She asked us a question from deep within her soul, "Are there any men who are trustworthy?"

We answered, "Yes." And we believe there are just as many trustworthy men as there are women.

First you must trust yourself.

This may sound obvious, but there's more to it than you think. Shira was convinced that she trusted herself, and was also convinced that she couldn't trust Bryce. She didn't realize, however, just how much she ignored her intuition, gave him her power, and then felt betrayed by him. How did this happen? She got pregnant early in their relationship. Although she was in an emotional turmoil, she recognized a deep place within her that wanted the baby. She told Bryce that she wanted the baby, but also told him she couldn't think clearly. So she asked him to make the decision for her. He chose abortion, and that's what they did. The emotional pain of this decision never left her, and she could never shake the feeling of betrayal by Bryce.

We helped Shira see the betrayal of herself by giving her power over to Bryce. This was a big mistake. Rather than trust her own intuition, even though her mind was not clear, she chose instead to trust Bryce. Although Bryce has often apologized for choosing the abortion, it has not been enough. We asked Shira to make two apologies, one to Bryce for giving him her own authority and, the main one, to herself for ignoring her intuition and how much she wanted the baby.

She was able to make these two apologies, and it made a significant difference in their relationship. She realized that, whenever she trusted herself first, she was then able to trust Bryce.

I've also watched Joyce's trust in me grow as she has learned to trust herself. Sometimes, my personal desires have caused me to try to get my own way with Joyce. One time stands out from years ago. I wanted to take Joyce and one-year-old Rami to a remote lake while we were staying near Mt. Shasta. Joyce didn't have a good feeling about it, but let my enthusiasm overrule her intuition. I drove our VW bus on roads that would have been a challenge in a four-wheel-drive vehicle. Halfway to the lake, the clutch cable snapped. It took most of the day to drive without a clutch, mostly in first gear, back to the house.

Yes, her trust in me took a hit. But she eventually realized that she hadn't trusted herself, and the bad feeling she had from the first moment of saying yes to me.

Now, she listens carefully to her intuition. She trusts herself. Consequently, I feel much more deeply trusted by her, even when I make mistakes. An example is our river trips, which are more important to me than to Joyce, but she also enjoys them for the most part. As long as she listens to her intuition moment by moment, and gets a yes, she goes on these trips with me. We have gone through some big rapids where she has been scared at times but, even then, she still listens to her intuition first. This past summer I made a mistake that caused the raft to flip, an ordeal that lasted half the day and ended our trip prematurely. It would have been natural for Joyce to trust me less as a river guide but, because her intuition did not alert her, she still trusts me. It did help that I learned a great deal from the mishap, minimizing the likelihood that it would happen again. But it's a great feeling that my wife trusts me so deeply.

But there was a larger issue. How is it possible for Joyce to trust me after I had an affair with her best friend after three years of marriage? By all rights, she should still be shaky in her trust. But she trusts me completely with other women. Before this act of betrayal, I loved Joyce but was in denial of my need for her. I was in denial of my inner little boy who needed love. Because she now sees and feels my inner child's need for her love, she knows I have absolutely no desire or need to cross a boundary with another woman. She trusts my need for her. She trusts me completely.

Trust him by being vulnerable with him.

If you vulnerably show a man your need for his love, he will feel trusted by you, and will want to do everything he can to live up to that trust. If you show your need for his love without also showing your vulnerability, you risk coming across in a condescending way, like a demanding mother to a son. This will not communicate your trust. Quite the contrary, it probably will communicate that you have little trust in him.

We often hear from women, "I'll be vulnerable with him when he shows me that I can trust him." This attitude doesn't work. Your vulnerability opens the door to trust. You will only find out how trustworthy he is when you show him your vulnerability. It is your weakness, your fear, or the trembling heart of the little girl, that fully empowers him as a nurturer ... that causes him to eagerly step up as your protector.

Okay, there are exceptions. If he is an addict and not in recovery, or suffering from a mental illness, or abusing you physically or emotionally, it may not be safe for you to be vulnerable. It may not be appropriate for you to trust him if you live in one of these situations. But for most men, your vulnerability will work like a charm.

Also, you don't have to trust him in every area of life. If he barely knows how to boil water, you don't have to trust him to prepare a gourmet meal for you. Nor do you need to trust him to prune your prize rosebushes. Joyce doesn't trust me to do this either. And I don't trust her to prune my fruit trees. Yes, some things are hers and some things mine.

But, for the relationship to be strong, you need to trust him in important ways. Joyce trusts me to be there when she really needs me. When we lost our third pregnancy, Joyce needed to completely lean on my strength. She collapsed into a well of grief and pain. Yes, it was my baby too, and I had my own grief, but Joyce trusted me to still be strong for her. And the depth of her vulnerability and need for my love drew a strength out of me that I didn't even know I had. Her trust made me more trustworthy.

Joyce trusts me to safely hold her inner little girl. When she is feeling sad or afraid, she knows she can come to me and ask me to hold her. She trusts that I will drop anything I am doing in the moment to hold and comfort that precious little girl within her. Again, it's her vulnerable need for love that powerfully opens my heart and arms.

Joyce trusts me with our children. When they were little, she knew I let them take bigger risks than she did. On river trips, if they wanted to jump off high rocks into the river, I first made sure it was safe, then gave them my full encouragement. Joyce might have preferred they jump from lower heights, but she trusted my judgment. Now that our children are grown, Joyce trusts that I can help them in unique ways, not just physically or mentally, but emotionally as well.

Joyce trusts me to keep myself safe on my adventures. She trusts that I take the most conservative routes through rapids, especially when I travel alone in the wilderness, and a rescue could be a long time in coming.

Joyce trusts me as a healer. Sometimes she asks me to place my hands on some part of her body that hurts her, and just send light and healing energy into her body. She trusts that she can receive something from me that she can't from any other health practitioner.

Joyce trusts me as a therapist and teacher. When we work together, whether we're seeing one person or one couple, or a room full of people in a workshop, I feel her look to me with immense trust. Sometimes, there are difficult situations to handle and, even though Joyce is every bit as competent and experienced, she trusts that I bring something unique to the situation. It is so good to feel her confidence in me.

Most important to me, Joyce trusts my connection with my Higher Power. She knows I have a different approach to spirituality than she has, but she trusts that I am every bit as spiritual as she is. Sometimes, she is upset about something at bedtime, and will ask me to say a prayer to help her sleep. I usually ask the angels to enfold her in their loving arms of light so she may be able to sleep peacefully through the night. She loves this, and usually sleeps through the whole night because of my prayer.

When a man feels trusted by you, he feels loved. He feels important, needed and wanted. This is a great feeling for most men.

Trust Practice

> Write down 10 ways that you trust your man. It may surprise you how many ways you do trust him.
>
> Show him the list but, even better, tell him in your own words.

To Really Love the Little Boy Inside the Man

NO MATTER HOW BIG A MAN IS, THERE LIVES WITHIN HIM A SMALL BOY. No matter how powerful, inside him dwells a powerless child. No matter how confident, his inner child needs reassurance. And no matter how loving, that little boy yearns for your love.

We, as men, often learn early in our lives to pretend we're stronger than we really are. We painfully learn that we are not really safe in this world. Whereas, usually, girls suffer verbal assaults from peers, boys often have the added factor of physical as well as verbal assaults. I have a vivid memory of standing in the schoolyard in Brooklyn, New York. I was either five or six years old. Another little boy approached me and, without the slightest warning, punched me in the stomach. It was a direct blow to my solar plexus, and I crumpled to the ground, gasping for breath, terrified that I was about to die.

Yet the little boy within the man endures so much more than fear of physical violence. When boys are criticized too much, and even a little bit of criticism can be too much, it damages their self-esteem, and you can have a man who feels he can never get it right, no matter how hard he tries. When boys are controlled too much, they need to rebel when they get older, and too often this can last a whole lifetime. So many men clearly express their need for respect from their partner, but how many are unaware that it's really the child within that felt disrespected growing up.

The Hidden Inner Child

Perry and Selma have quite a story. When Selma asked for a divorce after twenty-four years of marriage, Perry insisted they first try counseling. Selma reluctantly agreed, so Perry, a psychiatrist, got recommendations from his colleagues for a psychiatrist he didn't know personally. It was a disaster. Selma felt manipulated and bullied. Perry chose another psychiatrist. Selma left mid-session. Exasperated, Perry finally agreed to let Selma choose the counselor. She chose Joyce and me.

We were not prepared for what was about to happen. Perry walked into our office first and looked at our walls. "Where are your diploma and license?" he immediately and brusquely asked.

"Put away somewhere," was my somewhat lame reply.

Joyce started to say hello to him but he ignored her, turned back to me, and proceeded to list his wife's psychiatric diagnoses. I think there were three. Meanwhile, Selma quietly slipped into the room and was greeted lovingly by Joyce.

When the four of us were seated, Perry once again took command and outlined Selma's problems, complete with her past history from childhood, psychiatric symptoms, and with a final flair, her mental status examination. Selma sat timidly, but her eyes looked to us, pleading for help.

As Perry took a breath, I butted in, "Perry, we need to let Selma speak."

"Fine," he blurted out, clearly unhappy about giving up any control.

Selma hesitantly began, "See what I have to put up with. He treats me like a patient. Wait. That's not right. Even his patients get better treatment than I do. At least he cares about them. I feel so unloved, and to be honest, right now I can't even love myself. I feel trapped in the marriage and powerless to do anything, including leaving."

While Selma spoke, I couldn't help notice Perry out of the corner of my eye. Absentmindedly, he ran his finger along a ledge of trim on the wall behind the couch, a ledge that probably hadn't been dusted in years. Then he looked with a mildly disgusted expression at the black dust coating his finger.

Either ignoring or not noticing his evaluation of our office, Joyce asked Perry, "What is your part, Perry? How do you contribute to the problems in the relationship?"

Unbelievably, Perry made no eye contact with Joyce. After all, she was only a nurse with a master's degree. Instead, he looked at me, the MD, and continued his treatise about Selma, even though we interrupted him repeatedly to try to get him to take any responsibility for their marital problems.

At long last, he conceded that he didn't give Selma enough of his time and, just maybe, he was too hard on her.

As they walked out at the end of the hour, Selma discreetly mouthed the words "thank you" to Joyce.

Selma made the next appointment with us, even though Perry tried to convince her we were not professional enough. The second session went a little better. Perry realized he couldn't get away with being the psychiatrist in their own marriage.

In the third session, we steered Perry into the dysfunction of his own childhood, which he was willing to divulge, albeit a bit clinically. By now, we had achieved some degree of Perry's trust, and perhaps complete trust from Selma. We made our move. Reflecting back to them how unbalanced their relationship appeared on the surface, with him being the father and she the little girl, we announced our intention to reveal the opposite dynamic. We asked Perry to lay his head on Selma's lap and let her hold him the way a mother would hold a little boy.

By the expression on his face, you'd think we were asking him to repeat first grade. Again, he looked only at me,

"I don't have time for this nonsense. I'm an important man."

I asked him, "Perry, do you want to save your marriage or not?"

With a grunted, "Oh, all right," he laid his head on Selma's lap and barked, "Now what?"

We asked him again to speak about his childhood, which he again did more as a psychiatrist than as a client.

Then, the miracle happened. Joyce leaned close and put her hand on his heart, and gently asked, "What hurt you the most in your childhood?"

We could actually see his mind come to a grinding halt as something deeper took over. More than Joyce's question, it was her hand on his chest that seemed to be the magic ingredient. A tear slowly slipped down from one of Perry's eyes as he said, "I can't ever remember being touched or held as a child. It just wasn't right. I got plenty of praise for my intellectual achievements, but I honestly can't remember any real caring. Now that I actually feel my childhood, it feels shallow and empty, devoid of what was really important ... love."

Finally, the dam broke and the tears flowed freely.

Selma was crying too while she stroked his head and face.

We asked her to speak to Perry, so she did, straight from her heart. "This is the first time you've ever shown me this part of you, this wonderful part of you, your vulnerability, and the real pain of your childhood. I feel like you're allowing me in for the first time. You're beautiful to me right now. I'd given up all hope of ever seeing your beauty, your depth."

She pulled his head up against her heart and gently rocked him while they both cried. Then Perry looked up at Selma and said, "Now I know how to make our marriage work. I'm sorry I never knew how."

We continued our work with Selma and Perry for a few months. Something huge had shifted in their relationship, and they dove headlong into the work of recapturing the elusive mother-son bond of love. Something symbolically big had shifted as well with the four of us. It became difficult to get Perry to look at me. He only wanted to look at Joyce. Now she had become a symbol of the hidden source of mothering wisdom and love he had missed his whole life. I had my merits, but Joyce, and of course Selma, were what he needed most.

They went on a two-week cruise together to renew their vows of marriage. And we received thank you cards from different parts of the world over the next year.

> *Julie leaves little love notes in my billfold especially when she knows I'm going to have a really hard day. I feel really special, that she really cares about my needs.*
> –Paul Olson, San Rafael, CA

How Joyce Loves my Inner Little Boy

There have been times when Joyce has been holding me and I have spoken about the violence in my childhood and adolescence. She has spoken words that go right through to the deepest part of me, words that I have always needed to hear, words that allow me to feel safe and completely loved. She says with the utmost tenderness, "I can't promise you, Barry, that I'll never get angry at you, but I can promise that I will never hurt your body."

Joyce has spoken these words to me a number of times, but I can never get tired of hearing them. The little boy inside me needs to know that I am completely safe with at least one person. Joyce has at times gotten angry with me since we first met in 1964, and she has said hurtful things to me just as I have said hurtful things to her, but she has never hurt my body. Yes, her words have hurt me, sometimes deeply, but we always work through these difficulties to resolution. The child part of me isn't so much afraid of hurtful words. He's more afraid of being hit. So Joyce's reassurance that she will never, ever hurt my body, is just the comfort my inner child needs. It gives me the safety to be more present when the two of us are angry at each other, rather than running away, either physically or emotionally. My inner child actually trusts that Joyce will never hit me. And even more important, he is realizing that he never deserved to be hit … for anything!

I admit, I'm much better at fathering Joyce's little girl than asking for the mothering I need from her. I feel great joy whenever I can hold her as a little girl, but this can easily get out of balance. When our unborn third child died after six months of pregnancy, I became the strong father who took care of my deeply grieving wife. I held her and comforted her day after day. I helped more with our two girls, Rami and Mira. It felt good to be so deeply needed, but after about a month I found myself less and less able to be present and strong for Joyce. We were drifting apart as a couple.

One day, Joyce asked if she could hold me as a child. I lay in her lap and listened as she spoke, "Barry, I'm not the only one who lost a baby. Please allow me to comfort you, and allow yourself to feel your own grief."

That simple invitation was all that was needed. I put my strong father self aside and was able to feel my sadness, my helplessness, my grief. I could at last be a small child in Joyce's capable and loving arms. Balance was restored to our relationship, and we were close again.

Like I said, staying with and feeling my inner child is a lifelong quest. It is part of my spiritual quest. Whenever I feel my inner child's need for love, I also feel my soul's need for God. If I keep my inner child hidden, I am also hiding my need for the Great Source of Love. But I forget this truth daily. Sometimes I'll get stuck in my head. I'll make myself too busy. I'll lose touch with my feelings, especially my need for love and my need for Joyce. But Joyce, bless her heart, has learned a great trick that she has passed along to many other women. When she sees me disconnected from my heart, she will ask permission to gently rub the center of my chest. How could I ever say no to a request like that? I almost never have. As she rubs my heart area, I'm just like a cat. It doesn't take long for my heart motor to purr. Ahhhh! I remember who I am. Life is good again!

One important reminder here. For too many couples, touch is equated with sex. There is not enough non-sexual touch and holding that doesn't lead to sex. Many people, especially women, have expressed their fear about doing a practice like rubbing their partner's heart, or even the parent-child holding exercise. They fear that any physical touching or holding will sexually arouse their partner, or will lead to the expectation of sex. So, they withhold all touch, but everybody loses here. Instead, make clear your own need for non-sexual touch, the sacred touch between a child and parent. Make time for this in your relationship, and you will see that, other times, your sexual relationship will be even more fulfilling. (For more on non-sexual touch, see "Please Just Hold Me" in *To Really Love a Woman*)

Inner Practice

Think of the man you love. Can you visualize his face? Can you see past his adult face to his childlikeness?

If this is difficult, look through his childhood photos and pick out several that show that sweet innocent child. Frame these and put them on your dresser to be looked at each day.

Imagine the suffering he most likely went through growing up, the criticism, the rejection or abandonment, or the physical or emotional abuse.

Now imagine comforting that child or adolescent, holding him with love and safety, holding him like you would your own small child.

Relationship Practice

Hold the man you love the way a parent would hold a little boy.

Let him know he is safe. He doesn't have to protect himself or you in this moment. Encourage him to really let down his guard.

Give him permission to talk about and feel his fears, his pain, and his sadness. Give him permission to go back into his childhood and revisit painful memories. Tell him you will be there with him, holding him.

Listen to him. Give him time in silence to go inside and then form words.

Acknowledge and validate him. Speak to him as a loving parent, giving him the messages he most needed to hear as a child.

To Really Make Love to a Man

WHEN I WAS A YOUNGER WOMAN IN MY EARLY THIRTIES, I was leading a women's retreat and, spontaneously, the subject of sex was brought up. One of the participants, Sherrie, was upset with her husband because he didn't please her sexually, at least in the way she wanted. She shared with the group that they often got into fights over this, and she felt like leaving him. I looked around the group of women and noticed Barbara, a woman in her seventies, who had shared that she had a wonderful fifty-five-year relationship with her husband. I stopped Sherrie and asked Barbara if she had something to say. What she said has stayed with me to this day, "I tell my husband every single day that his lips really turn me on. Then we have a long and wonderful kiss." She smiled and seemed so content, then she continued, "I want my husband to know every single day that he is still handsome and sexy in my eyes. He repays this appreciation with abounding love and attention to me."

What I hear in Barbara's words are the messages: "Concentrate on the positive. Every day find something … anything … to appreciate about your man's sexuality."

Sherrie looked to the floor and remarked that she had never appreciated her husband's sexuality. She had been so concentrated on how he could improve that she had never appreciated him. She made an important decision in that moment, "I want to go home and try again with my husband. I want to appreciate all the ways that he does try to satisfy me."

A year later, I heard from Sherrie again. She and her husband were doing much better together. As she appreciated his sexuality, he in turn became more open to listening to how he could more deeply please her. But she didn't have much to ask. Just by her appreciation, her husband became the more sensitive lover she needed.

Leaving that women's retreat, I decided to take Barbara's words to heart. Every day, in some creative way, I have appreciated some aspect of Barry's sexuality. I let him know that I find him very attractive. Even though he is now very much a senior, I tell him that he is more handsome than ever and that I am so attracted to him. I tell him that I love the feel of his lips upon mine and love to feel his warm and tender hugs. His body has changed from the eighteen-year-old with whom I fell passionately in love, yet I run my hands over his body every day, an act that never fails to please him. And I tell him how much I love his body and how the changes are even more appealing to me. Barry has wrinkles now on his face and I tell him that they cause his kisses to be even more sensual. Sometimes I say the same things every day, but from the smile on his face I know he never grows weary of my remarks. Barry knows I love his sensuality, and that has allowed this sensuality to be expressed in a sensitive and loving way.

It's important for couples to communicate lovingly about their sexual relationship. This subject needs more love and tenderness than perhaps any other. It hurts a man deeply when his partner compares him negatively to past sexual partners. This happened to Bill and Jasmine. Bill felt so devastated to be compared negatively to other men, that eventually he couldn't have sex with Jasmine at all. Their relationship ended in divorce.

We were able to follow Bill's progress for many years after the divorce. At first, he was afraid to be with another woman. Then he met a compassionate woman who was able to help him heal from the negative comments and comparisons. He has since had a fulfilling relationship with her.

We have also been able to follow Jasmine's progress over these years and have seen her in many different relationships. She has continued her destructive behavior of negatively comparing current partners to other men who have pleased her sexually, and each relationship ends within the first year.

Sexuality is an area where a couple needs to give a lot of positive energy. However, not all men and women know exactly how to please their partner sexually. That is why it is important to communicate in a loving way with your partner. There have been times in my relationship with Barry when it has been important to communicate with him, because what he was doing no longer felt good to me. I would say something like, "Barry dear. That doesn't feel so good right now, but here's what would feel great... How could I expect him to know about changes in my body without my telling him?

One of these times was when I was pregnant with our first child. A lot of women just give up having sex while they are pregnant because it sometimes doesn't feel good. However, with loving communication, a way can be found that feels good to both of you. I remember that, with experimenting, we found such a way, and continued having sex right up until several weeks before Rami was born. We both enjoyed these times very much.

Barry has always had more sexual energy than I have had. When we were first married, I felt a little overwhelmed by how often he wanted to have sex. I would usually say yes, because I thought as a good wife I needed to love Barry in this way. Usually my heart was into it, but sometimes it wasn't. If I had sex with Barry when I didn't really want to, I wouldn't feel good afterwards. Rather than the usual close happy time afterwards, I would feel irritable with him. So I started saying no when I didn't want to have sex. But I felt I really didn't have a right to say no and, by the time the no would come out to Barry, it would carry the negative force of guilt. Barry would feel rejected and there would be distance between us. Then, the next time he approached me sexually, I would say yes even though I didn't want to, just to avoid the distance.

As you can see, this pattern was dysfunctional. Finally I got it. I needed to love myself just as much as I loved Barry, and that included honoring the times I did not want sexual closeness. I learned to say no with as much love as I would have said yes. If Barry wanted to have sex with me and, for whatever reason, it just wasn't right for me, I learned to reach out and hug him tight, acknowledge his affections, and tell him it just wasn't the right time for me. I might even suggest we do something else together. I got to say the no I needed, and Barry didn't feel rejected. He felt me saying no to sex, but more importantly he felt me saying yes to him and to love. We were able to go on and have a close time. Then when I would say yes to sex, Barry knew I really meant it and those times were always powerful and beautiful.

Sometimes Barry really wants to have sex, is aroused and ready to go. I feel close to him but feel no sexual energy whatsoever. At these times I feel like he is miles ahead of me and I could never catch up, but I would like to be experiencing what he is feeling. Rather than just say no to him, I give him the challenge, "Can you bring me to where you are?" Barry loves this opportunity to romance me. Usually he rubs my back, kisses me lightly, tells me what he loves about me, and sometimes sings to me. I love these special times, and Barry loves this opportunity to pour his love into me. It doesn't matter how long it takes, he enjoys awakening the sensual goddess in me.

At the close of every time of lovemaking, whether it ends with an orgasm or not, I always tell Barry how much I love him and how beautifully he pleases me. I let him know he is the most wonderful lover in the world. I want him to know that I am so attracted to him and love joining with him sexually. I want him to know that he brings me so much joy. I hold him close and tell him that the best decision I ever made was to marry him.

Barry: Joyce and I are convinced men and women equally crave the sublime ecstasy of sexual joining. Although it may appear that a man and a woman have different desires for sex, we both long for that delicious union during lovemaking where minds and egos cease to be in control, where we can drift together on a vast sea of eternal love, where it is no longer he or she, but it becomes a heavenly *us*. We both want the nectar of heightened sexual feelings to flow into every part of our lives, to be there long before the actual physical sexual act, and to last long after.

That said, men often have specific sexual needs and desires, ways they are turned on and feel loved by their partner. For you to truly understand how to turn him on, not just superficially, but to really turn him on, to open his heart along with his body, is to give him a great gift of love.

I love the sound of Joyce's voice. Her loving words have the power to open my heart in most circumstances. But I have to admit, I love her touch even more. Her hands have the ability to directly channel her heart's love into my body and soul. I love it when she spontaneously touches me, and I usually welcome her touch anywhere on my body. She also knows that, when we're walking together (which we often do with our dogs), it means so much to me when she reaches for my hand. She holds my hand or touches me because her hands say "I love you" in a direct way.

And when we are making love, she has learned the kind of touch that makes all the difference for me, most importantly the when, the where, and the how much. This has required communication and experimentation. And it is still up to me to keep communicating my need regarding specific touch. She can't always read my mind.

Joyce also loves me sexually by her receptivity. I feel that my loving words and actions are deeply taken in by her. Her receptivity lets me know that I am important to her. Her body and feelings become an open vessel into which I can pour my adoration. This is so much deeper than a penis filling a vagina. True receptivity is not passive. It is, on the contrary, an active way of giving love, but not necessarily obvious or visible. It's the way Joyce's body becomes sensually alive in response to a true act of love on my part. I can feel her body open like a flower when I describe the ways she is a goddess or when I sing my love to her.

She loves me sexually by knowing the exact moment to stop giving to me, and thus allowing me to give to her. This can be when I'm becoming too aroused and she feels she needs to catch up. One of her favorite things to do at that moment is ask me to gently caress her back for a few minutes. It gives me a chance to pour my love into her body through my hands. I know from experience the exact kind of touch she loves, but I also love to experiment with new and different kinds of touch. The soft sounds coming from her mouth let me know when I'm on track.

Joyce loves me sexually by letting me lead, by letting me be powerful – not more powerful, but just as powerful as she is. She is the most powerful woman I have ever met, but she knows how to relinquish control and pass the torch to me. If I abuse this gift of power in any way, if I try to get her to do things she doesn't feel comfortable with, she will tense and come back into control. So I hold this gift of power as sacred, and lead with the utmost respect and care.

Joyce loves me sexually by appreciating me as a lover. I sometimes feel overwhelmed by the mastery she ascribes to me. I don't feel like a master of sex by any means, but in her eyes I am, and this feels so good.

Besides being a master of receptivity, Joyce also takes the lead at times. She knows how to ask for what she wants, which makes me happy. She may need more words from me if I've been silent too long, and she'll ask for this with happy anticipation that empowers me to speak my love, rather than with guilt or negativity that would kill the love. Rather than saying, "You're too quiet, Barry," she will say something like, "Your loving words right now would feel so good." See the difference.

Joyce understands that I, like many men, like spontaneity and creativity in our lovemaking. There is the somewhat crude adage, "A woman needs a reason to make love. A man only needs a place." While the feeling of connection and intimacy is truly important to both sexes, many men feel loved when their partner suggests something different, something new or creative, or initiates sex in places other than the bedroom. I remember making love on a remote beach with the sound of the pounding waves, the delicious feeling of the warm sun on our naked bodies. It was spontaneous. It was different. It was amazing! Then I looked up and saw a troop of Boy Scouts marching by with their adult leader, trying so hard not to look at us. We scrambled to find our clothes and cover up, then both of us started laughing. It didn't matter that we were interrupted. It was wonderful!

> *I feel so loved by you Karla when you spontaneously play or dance with me even after all these years.*
> –Rob Gitlin, Redwood Valley, CA

Sexual Moments

Joyce: At least once a day we have what we call a "sexual moment." These moments usually consist of a warm and loving kiss, and holding each other a little longer and more passionately than usual. They can happen at any time that we are alone. We have an agreement between us that, while we have these sensual moments, even if we get aroused (or more typically, Barry), we don't have to "do" anything about it right then. Sometimes, if our children were out of the room playing, we would stop making dinner, go into the bathroom, and have a passionate embrace. Sometimes the sexual moment would just last a minute or two, but we would both enjoy it and it would give us energy and joy.

In these moments, I would always tell Barry how much I love him and how much I love his body. I would also tell him how much I was looking forward to the next time we could be together sexually. Sometimes that next time didn't happen for several days, but these sexual moments bring enthusiastic anticipation. We make these moments light as well as passionate, joyful and full of laughter as well as sexual. If days go by and we don't have one of our sexual moments, we know we have gotten off balance.

When we were eighteen and dating each other, these sexual moments were more like sexual hours. When our children were small our sexual moments were more like a minute or two. Now that our children are grown and not living at home, our sexual moments can take on any length of time we desire.

The important thing though is that they are just what they are; they are not the full sexual activity. Sometimes Barry gets carried away into a more focused sexual energy. Then I have permission to tease him and let him know he is in what we have affectionately termed "the zone," which is his reminder that this is just a "moment," not foreplay. He's great about backing off a little to cool down.

These sexual moments have brought immeasurable joy and fulfillment to both of us. They have allowed us to keep our sexual energy alive each day.

> *I feel especially loved by Jane in the middle of the dance floor with people all around us and she'll lean into me in a very intimate tango embrace, as if I were the only person in the whole room.*
> –Ron, Las Vegas, NV

Barry: You need to know that a sexual moment is a wonderful gift to most men. Even if we get lost momentarily in "the zone," and want the whole enchilada, please know it won't hurt us physically to stop. As I say to many audiences of couples, "Erections subside without any ill effects." True, the ache described as "blue balls" usually is the result of a long time of arousal, not minutes. A sexual moment (or minutes) will have no harmful physical effects upon a man.

Psychologically, it may be hard for him to stop, as Joyce mentioned above about me. That's why it's so important to have a mutual agreement beforehand. Both of you must agree that the purpose of these sexual moments is to keep awake your sexual energy and connection. Our sexual moments feel so good to me, I naturally want to prolong them. The moment Joyce announces that it's enough, I honor our agreement and allow myself to cool down. There have even been a few times that I have been the one to stop first (okay, very few).

You are NOT being a tease when you have a clear agreement about sexual moments. You are not being cruel or torturing him. Instead, you are allowing sexual energy and momentum to be felt on a continuing basis. If he makes this agreement for sexual moments, but then pressures you for more and then gets angry when it doesn't come, he has broken his agreement and you have a problem. Sexual moments cannot work for you as a couple without a clear agreement.

Too many couples go for days or even weeks without any sexual feeling or arousal, then expect to make love on a moment's notice. For many women, sexual energy goes dormant with time. The more time that goes by, the deeper the sleep of the sexual goddess. Explain this to your man. Let him know these sexual moments keep the goddess in a lighter sleep, so when the time comes for making love, your sexual energies are closer to the surface. Let him know sexual moments are romantic.

[More on sexual moments in *To Really Love a Woman*]

Sexual Communication: What You Appreciate

Sacred sexuality starts with the desire to bring more love into your sexuality. It starts with communicating with your partner. Please don't assume I am writing about some advanced tantric teaching that is almost impossible to master. Joyce and I want very much to make sacred sexuality attainable to everyone.

In our couple's workshops, we have each person communicate with their partner about sexuality in two ways. First we invite them to appreciate or acknowledge something beautiful about their sexual relationship. There is perhaps no area of relationship that needs appreciation more. Some of the deepest wounds in relationship have occurred because of sexual criticism, or comparing someone unfavorably with a previous partner. There is always something good to be appreciated. Most couples simply don't take the time to acknowledge the goodness of their sexuality as a couple, or the goodness of their partner's sexuality.

For example, in *To Really Love a Woman*, there is a small section called "The Myth of Penis Size." Men often have anxiety about the size of their penis, whether too big or too small, linking size to their ability to please you. The man you love may or may not have some of this anxiety, but to sincerely appreciate the size of his penis may help him very much. And he may never ask for this specific appreciation.

Each of you take as much time as you need to appreciate the beauty of any part of your sexual relationship or your partner's sexuality. Take turns with this, each of you addressing one thing at a time. Remember specific times of lovemaking that were special. Describe to your lover the specific things they did that really turned you on. Once you begin this dialogue, you may not want it to end. That's how important it is.

Sexual Communication: What You Need

Now, let your man know what you need to be more deeply fulfilled sexually. This is not an opportunity to tell him what he is doing wrong. Rather, it is a time to give him vital information about *yourself*. Please be sensitive. There are certain things he may not feel comfortable doing. This is not a time to put pressure on him to do what you want.

If you want, start the practice by completing these two statements:
It really turns me on when you _____.
I feel really loved when you _____.

These kinds of statements empower your partner rather than criticize them.

Loving a Man by Taking Care of Your Body

Most men (remember, not all men) are more focused than women on the physical side of lovemaking. The appearance of our woman is often more important than we care to admit.

True, the sex center in the brain, the hypothalamus, is larger in men than in women, and we have more testosterone, but this is not the only reason. It's our upbringing too. We are often trained from adolescence to have a sexual response to visual images of women.

You love your man by taking care of your body. This does not mean you have to look like a young Hollywood actress, who often has to starve herself to be that thin. (Although it appears Hollywood is finally getting the message. More and more stars are looking like the rest of us.) No, you love your man by keeping yourself as fit and healthy as you can.

Joyce has gained some weight as she ages, but she takes care of her body. She eats healthy food and she exercises every day. Of course she does this more for herself, but she knows it's also an act of love toward me. Her body is beautiful to me. I love to see her without clothes, and she knows it. I love the feel of her curves. She knows how much I love to touch her. She keeps a "lover's body" by her constant care.

What about clothes? Joyce knows I like to see her in clothes that show off her body. Her temptation, though, was to wear loose-fitting clothes. Then, on our annual work trips to Europe, she noticed women actually showing off their bodies by the clothes they were wearing, regardless of how much they weigh. European women appeared to be less obsessed by the image of the "perfect" body. So Joyce started wearing clothes that defined her curves. I felt this, and still do, as an act of love toward me.

If you, as a woman, want to fully love your man, take care of your body. It's not enough to love him in all the other things you do for him. Of course, taking care of your body is a way to more fully love yourself, but it is also a practical way to love him. You may feel frustrated and hopeless about getting into shape by yourself. Just don't stop there. Get the help you need. Most of the time, it's simply your shame that keeps you from getting help. Make it fun. Fitness machines may not be your thing, but a dance or yoga class may be just the ticket. Joyce loves swimming, and swims for an hour most every day, in addition to walking our dogs.

And remember, it's not about the "perfect" body. It's about the "lover's" body. The "lover's" body can carry extra pounds, or be too thin, or have the "wrong" proportions. The "lover's" body is developed for making love, just as much with the eyes of your beloved as with his body. The "lover's" body is an attitude, an intention, the way you hold yourself, and the way you show yourself off. Clothes or no clothes, Joyce has a playfully seductive way of pausing on her way through the room when she sees me looking at her. She smiles, winks, tilts one of her hips, and proudly throws her shoulders back. It's playful. It's provocative. It's a moment of showing her love to her man.

Challenges to Sexually Loving a Man

Life can present obstacles to making love to a man. But no obstacle is too big to be surmounted if there is enough love and persistence. Take Donna and Ron Sturm for example. They have given us permission to tell their remarkable story, using their real names, with the hope that other couples will be helped through seeming insurmountable sexual obstacles. Ron developed prostate cancer and, as sometimes happens after surgery, he completely lost the ability to have an erection. To make matters even worse, he was put on female hormones to further treat the cancer. So not only was he unable to physically function sexually, but he also had no desire. His libido was eliminated by the estrogen.

Donna, however, refused to give up on their sexual relationship. She asked herself, "What if the situation was reversed? What if I were the one who lost my sexual desire and function? What would I need from Ron?"

She marched into the bedroom where Ron was resting and sat down on the side of the bed next to her husband. "Ron, honey," she began, "please allow me to make love to you."

A look of surprise came over Ron's face, then it turned to sadness as he said, "Donna, you know I can't do that."

Donna remained steadfast, "I know you can't Ron, but I still want to give to you. Please just lie there and receive my love."

She then gently opened his pants and took his shrunken penis in her hands, and then her mouth. In that moment, the size of Ron's penis didn't matter to Donna. His sexual prowess was unimportant. All that mattered was how much she loved her wonderful man, and that maybe, just maybe, her love could somehow quicken his healing and recovery.

Ron, meanwhile, was moved to tears. In his words, "I couldn't believe how much Donna loved me. Without my own sexual energy and feelings, I was in that moment free to experience her pure love, her unconditional love. Without the sexual pleasure, I could feel an even deeper pleasure of being physically and non-physically adored. At first it was a challenge to just receive. So much of my ego and identity was wrapped up in how much I could give to Donna, but this was a new and truly remarkable experience. Instead of the orgasms that I was used to, I felt what I could only imagine to be a more feminine orgasm, involving all of me rather than one part of me. It was truly sublime!"

Donna continued her making love to Ron, and finally the miracle happened. One day, he felt a slight sensation of arousal, and his penis grew slightly in size. In the weeks and months that followed, his sexual response gradually returned to almost pre-surgery status. According to Ron, "I truly believe it was Donna's love and persistence, as well as God's grace, that caused the miracle."

The Two Sides of Impotence

Let's look at impotence. Impotence may be medically or psychologically attributed to one partner, but it cannot be overcome unless both partners take responsibility for each of their own parts. If one partner is blamed for impotence, then the "hidden impotence" of the other partner continues the dysfunction in the relationship.

Here's an example: Eliza blamed John for his impotence in their relationship. And John blamed himself as well. Looking only at the surface, it makes sense. John couldn't keep his erection. How could that have anything to do with Eliza? In our counseling sessions with them, we noticed that John was blamed for more than only unsatisfactory sex. In fact, he was blamed for everything that wasn't working in their relationship. He didn't make enough money. He didn't talk enough about his feelings. He wasn't spiritual enough.

When we asked Eliza to take responsibility for her own unhealthy contribution to their relationship, she first looked perplexed, then annoyed with us. She was, after all, an innocent victim, and she was unwilling to see that this position was her own "impotence." Blaming John for all the problems not only kept her from working on herself, but it kept her small and weak, in other words, impotent.

During one session, Joyce and I kept bringing the attention back to Eliza. We asked questions about her childhood. Eliza was, naturally, resistant to look at her own issues. But we gently persisted. When we finally saw tears in her eyes, we knew we were on track. We asked, "What are the tears about, Eliza?"

"There is something, but I don't want to talk about it."

We didn't say anything. We knew she just needed a little time.

With her eyes still closed, she finally said, "My mother did the same thing to my father!"

"What did she do?"

"The same thing I'm doing. My mother blamed everything on my father. She complained about him constantly to me. It hurt me so much because I knew some of the things were her fault. When I tried to speak up on his behalf, she always got angry at me, so I just stopped. I gave up on the truth. I stopped standing up for my father. And he still doesn't stand up for himself."

She started sobbing, while John, who had never seen his wife be so vulnerable, put his arm around her and pulled her close.

She let herself be held for a while, then sat back to look into his eyes and said, "I'm so sorry, John. I never understood how messed up my childhood was. I've hated the part of my mother that is so critical of my father, and I've turned out to be just like her. Now I hate that part of myself."

Her sobbing continued, and John pulled her close. She collapsed into his loving arms.

And yes, their relationship changed quickly after that session. Eliza learned how to recognize her lack of self-love, rather than blaming John. John learned to stand up more for himself. And the sexual relationship? Now that two people were working on their impotence – dramatically improved!

Menopause

Menopause can be a challenge in the area of sexuality. You may have less sexual desire because of hormonal changes. Vaginal dryness may make intercourse less pleasurable. You may be tempted to give up on sex altogether. You don't have to. Joyce didn't. She studied the research. She got the professional help she needed. To make better love to me, she kept letting me know that our sexual relationship was still very important to her. She also asked for what she specifically needed. Even so, for a period of time, it still hurt when I fully penetrated her. She invited me to penetrate gradually and slowly, stopping when she spoke her limit. She taught me new ways to pleasure her during this transition period.

Now, years later, her desire to make love with me is stronger than ever. She lets me know how much she looks forward to our next time of making love. Gone is the vaginal pain and dryness. I'm so glad she didn't give up on sex!

> *I feel really loved by you, Joyce, when you wrap your arms around me during a walk, draping yourself completely all over me, even hanging on me. It's a physical demonstration of your complete surrender to me and to love.*

Helping a Man to Play

A BEAUTIFUL WAY TO LOVE A MAN IS TO HELP HIM REMEMBER TO PLAY. Men can sometimes get overly serious with work, being the provider, worrying about investments, rising in their career, or perhaps getting their schooling. (Of course, these days, women can get just as serious but, because this book is about loving a man, we're focusing on him.)

For some men, sex is their only form of play. This is not enough. A healthy relationship also requires non-sexual forms of play.

Many of us have somehow forgotten the importance of play in our lives and relationships. We have concentrated upon "growing up" as fast as we could, equating maturity with seriousness and heaviness. But we can remember this forgotten art. Play can add a refreshing energy to a challenging situation. Smiles, a fun adventure or situation, giggles or a good hearty laugh can bring a gently healing energy and allow two people to get a different perspective, open their hearts and feel thankful once again for the friendship.

Healing can come through many different forms in relationship. The simple act of play can open doors between two people, begin a healing process, and bring profound changes.

Healing through play was illustrated to us quite dramatically several years ago through our cat, Rose. Eighteen years ago, I decided to go to the animal shelter to get a kitten for my father. My parents lived in an apartment above our garage and I felt a kitten would help my dad as he had recently become deaf. I found the perfect kitten at the shelter.

I was ready to leave with this new kitten when I walked by Rose's cage. She was around three years old and beautiful with her long white hair and one black spot. She was also visibly depressed with her nose to the far end of the cage. She had been there for a month. I wondered if her time was almost up. Something about her would not let me walk away.

I asked the volunteer about her and was told that she was becoming more depressed with each day, not moving and not looking at anyone. Something in me knew I had to give Rose a chance. I brought her home along with the kitten. Terrified, Rose quickly found our upstairs bathtub and would not move from it. (Fortunately, we have a separate shower, so the tub became Rose's shelter.) Only at night did she venture forth to eat and use the litter box. When we reached into the tub to pet her, she cowered as if she was afraid we would hit her. If we did touch her, she'd run to the other side of the bathtub.

This behavior went on for a month, and we were feeling we might never establish a relationship with her. We tried singing to her, sitting in the bathtub reading to her and offering special foods. She remained glued to her corner of the tub.

One evening our daughter, Mira, who was fourteen at the time, sat in the tub with Rose and began waving a cat toy in front of her. For ten minutes she sat, slowly swinging the toy with no response. Then a paw gingerly reached out and Rose began to play. She played with the cat toy and Mira for about fifteen minutes. Then she began to groom herself for the first time in over two months. The whole family gathered around the bathtub to watch, pride and joy radiating from our faces.

Each day, Mira sat by the bathtub and got Rose to play with various toys. Within a week, Rose let Mira pet her and even bring her to her bed. Seven months later, Rose had become one of our most affectionate cats. Playing seemed to bring memories of happier times in her life, and allowed her to open and trust us.

It is a well-known fact that children and young animals learn and grow through play. Adults also need to play and have fun. Sometimes, relationships can get so serious that the fun and joy get buried by all the talk. It is good to talk deeply and work things out, but this needs to be balanced with some amount of play.

During Barry's first year of medical school, he became serious. He was rejected by all the medical schools he applied to, but put on the waiting list for Meharry in Nashville, Tennessee. One week before school started, he received a notice that he was accepted and could start in one week. Since he was the last one admitted, he assumed he was the worst student in the class, and so he set about to study every minute that he could. He was strict about this, even though we had just gotten married in December of that first year. He told me he could be with me every Saturday afternoon, but no more than that.

After two weeks of that austere schedule, I felt it was wrong. I insisted that we have fifteen minutes each evening of play time. I asked that we could lie on our bed and just tickle each other, laugh at jokes or whatever. Reluctantly, he lay with me the first night, after first setting his timer for fifteen minutes. I started tickling him and, before he knew it, he was laughing and having a great time. This was not sexual, just fun like two little kids rolling around and giggling. We were playing. The timer went off after fifteen minutes. He turned it off and we continued to laugh for another fifteen minutes.

Then I suggested he get back to work and he did, but there was also a big smile on his face. We called it our play time and each and every school night we played and giggled, and it was so important. It helped to bring him through such a stressful year in which he thought he might fail, only to find out he was the number one student in the class. Personally, I think it was all the play that brought him those high grades.

Barry can also get serious around the computer, especially if it is not behaving. During these times, it looks as if a heavy weight is upon his shoulders. Rather than engaging him in discussions about the computer, of which I know comparatively little, I think of ways that we can play together just to change the energy, perhaps dancing in the living room, doing some gardening together or taking what I like to call "a gratitude and laughter walk." Usually, after playing and laughing for a bit, the reason that the computer isn't working will suddenly come to him in such clarity.

When our children were young and I sensed that Barry was getting overly serious about office matters, I would put on some lively music and we would all sneak into his office, tickle him and insist that he come into the living room to dance and play for a bit. He rarely refused and, when he returned to the office work, there was a bounce to his step.

Bringing laughter and fun is a beautiful way to love a man. You actually have a choice. You could criticize your man for being too serious. I don't think that would work very well. Or, you could invite him lovingly and laughingly into a "playground" of your making.

To Really Love a Man is to Love His Family

TO REALLY LOVE YOUR MAN IS TO MAKE AN EFFORT TO LOVE HIS FAMILY. Typically, men want to be connected to their families of origin. Occasionally, a man has been so wounded by his family that he needs to stay away, and then it would be important to support those feelings as well. If that is the case, then you could help him to feel a part of a healthy family with you. But if your man loves his family, then it is important to make an effort.

I know of two different situations where the man's wife does not like his family. In each case, she does not want anything to do with them. In one family, there is a mother, father and four grown children and their spouses, some of whom have children of their own. This particular family all gets together for Christmas each year, and it is the highlight of the year for them. The wife of one son refuses to come, even though her husband dearly wants to participate and they only live one hour away. Some years, he goes by himself to be with his family for Christmas, and some years he stays at home with her. But in either case he is unhappy. I know the members of this family and they are nice people. They have all gone out of their way to be close to his wife, but she does not want to be with them. All of the noise of their togetherness bothers her and she would rather be home alone in quiet.

Sometimes, loving our man means that we need to go beyond our comfort zone to participate with his family. I know that this was true for me. Barry's family was as different from mine as I could imagine. The only thing in common in both was that there was a lot of love. I liked my quiet family in which everyone listened when someone spoke. I liked the varied conversations around the dinner table and how my mother always tried to bring up inspiring subjects.

In Barry's family, everyone talked at the same time. In order to be heard, it was necessary to simply speak louder than everyone else. At every meal, there was shouting without anyone listening. The main subject of conversation was food. If Barry's dad cooked that particular meal, then it was necessary that everyone talk about the food he cooked while we were eating it. It was not enough to simply say, "This is delicious." There had to be a whole conversation about each dish. When we exhausted that subject, then the next meal was talked about. As a person who listens intently to conversations and finds it hard to ignore what people are saying, I tried to follow what each person was saying with sincerity ... tracking subjects, content, and feelings behind the words, all at the same time.

This is a gift that has eventually served me well as a therapist and group leader, but was difficult to have during these dinner conversations.

Barry learned to ignore it all and would just sit and eat his meal in his own bubble. I tried his approach of not listening but was unable to do so and soon was drawn in by the chaotic conversations and often found myself with a headache by the end.

Frankly, there were times that I wanted to withdraw from Barry's family altogether. I was not Jewish. Even though I knew that they liked me, still there was a prejudice toward non-Jewish people. I met Barry just twenty-one years after World War II and the Holocaust. Though my father was American, my grandfather came from Germany. There were times when their prejudice toward me hurt me, and I felt that I would do better just not being with Barry's family anymore. But he loved them! And so, in order to love Barry, I needed to find a way to make my peace with his family.

The first area I approached was the family meals, which were so important to them, especially his father. I found that instead of just listening to everyone talking at once, and Barry's dad shouting above the others because no one was really paying attention to the food that he cooked, I started to ask questions. The most effective question I asked was, "Please tell me how you made this dish?" Barry's dad loved this question, and would describe in detail how he made it. His face would light up as he was explaining how he chopped each vegetable and prepared each ingredient. Sometimes he even got out his knife and a fresh vegetable to illustrate his point.

The rest of the family quieted down and listened. Even Barry stopped ignoring what was happening and listened, picking up some valuable skills from his dad that have continued to serve him to this day. During these times of sharing his cooking secrets, Barry's dad seemed absolutely adorable to me. All he seemed to want was focused energy on his food. It seemed a simple thing to just give him this focused energy through questions.

Feelings and Boundaries

To get close to Barry's family, I also needed to be honest with my feelings and to set my own boundaries. This was difficult for me to do as I received little training in my own family on being honest with feelings that were bothering me. The first time I needed to do this was when Barry and I decided to get married. Neither set of parents was happy about this idea, but I believe that Barry's parents had the harder time. No one had ever married outside of the Jewish religion in their family. Being Jewish and raising Jewish children was a sacred responsibility to them.

One afternoon, as I was sitting outside alone in the backyard of Barry's parents' house, Barry's mom approached me and stood over me in a manner of authority.

Without any buildup or introduction, she simply blurted out, "I believe it is the responsibility of the woman to change for the man. You should become Jewish for Barry."

I was stunned that she would say such a thing and also by the abrupt way that she said it. There was silence as I looked at her and then I finally found my voice and said, "I can't do that for Barry and never will. My religion is very important to me."

She seemed unsure of what to say next, so she simply said, "Well, I've spoken my feelings in the hope that you would listen."

And I said, "I've spoken my feelings and hope that you will listen and that we won't have this conversation again." And with that, she walked away.

We never spoke about that time again. As a young, twenty-one-year-old woman, I was not used to standing up for myself around adults who were older than me. But I was grateful I did as it helped me in the future with Barry's mom.

The next big time I had to stand up for myself was when I was pregnant for the first time. We had just moved to Santa Cruz, California and were setting up our lives and psychotherapy practice. We were both excited about the possibility of having our first child. Barry's parents visited from New York. As soon as Barry's mom stepped into our home, she handed me a "gift." I opened it with eagerness expecting perhaps a gift for the baby. Inside was a book with the title, *How to Raise a Jewish Child*. I looked at the book for quite a time without opening it and then handed it back to her. With as much compassion and love as I could muster at the time, I told her I would not need this book. I gave her a hug and said, "We're going to raise this child in a different way." Stunned, she took the book away. That was the last time I had to set boundaries around religion with her.

During this same visit, I also had to confront Barry's dad. He had open-heart surgery several years previously, and that was all he would talk about ... except around meals, where the conversation still focused on food. When we would introduce him to our new friends, he would right away start telling them about his operation. After five days, I had had enough, as he had not once talked about the new baby. Through my tears, I expressed my hurt, "You don't in any way seem excited about your new grandchild."

I believe this was the first time that anyone had ever confronted Barry's dad. There was a silence in the room as I continued to cry softly. My words gave Barry the courage to share his own feelings, "Dad, it hurts me that you're so focused on your operation that happened two years ago, and don't show any interest in our pregnancy."

After another silence, Barry's mom spoke the most powerful words of all, "Michael, you're becoming a boring man."

Finally, Barry's dad spoke up, "I think you're right. I have become a boring man. I'm only thinking about myself.

I'm so sorry. I've been living my life in fear of another heart attack. I need to start living again." They left our home the next day.

Two weeks later, Barry's brother, Richard, called us. "What miracle did you do on Dad? He's a changed man. The spark is back in his life again and he's interested in other things again."

Barry's dad went on to live another twenty years until the dreaded fatal heart attack came. During that time, they moved to San Diego, California, where he went to college for the first time and completed his associate degree. They traveled extensively and he expanded his art career. He lived fully and the open-heart surgery was no longer the center of his world. I've had to confront him on several other occasions, sometimes with love but sometimes with anger. I truly believe my honesty with him allowed a deeper connection between us. I witnessed his growing respect and acceptance of me into the family.

When our first daughter was born, Barry called his parents right away to tell them the news. Barry's mom immediately asked, "Which side of the family does she look like?"

I'm sure she felt if the children were not going to be raised Jewish, at least they might look Jewish. Barry spoke the perfect words, even if they were not completely true, "She looks just like Joyce."

Barry's mom visited several weeks later and of course fell completely in love with our daughter. The fact that she didn't look Jewish and wasn't going to be raised Jewish no longer mattered. She loved Rami with the unconditional love of a grandmother. Through that love she also opened up to me in a way that she hadn't before. We began to bond in a beautiful way. She has been a wonderful grandmother to Rami as well as our other two children.

Though difficult in the beginning, I went on to have very satisfactory relationships with Barry's parents. Over the years, when they saw how happy Barry was in our marriage, they grew to totally accept me. Barry's dad continued to cook for us and give cooking tips until shortly before he died. I grew to have a deep and loving relationship with Barry's mom. I'm so grateful that I did not give up on being close with them. Barry has been grateful for all of my efforts with his parents and recognizes that it has all been done as an act of truly loving him. Every time I spoke with Barry's mom, I sincerely thanked her for raising a wonderful son and for her part in making him so loving. Even though I thanked her every time, she loved the appreciation and then always added, "You're the best thing that ever happened to Barry!"

Some tips for connecting with your man's parents

1. Thank them for raising such a wonderful son. Every parent needs to hear praise and gratitude, especially from the person who is married to or in partnership with their son.

2. Don't complain to his parents about things you do not like about him. If you are having difficulty with him, don't share it with his parents. It would be better to talk directly with your partner about the difficulty and, if you cannot get through it, then seek professional help.

3. It seldom happens that you will share a lot in common with your partner's parents. It is a blessing to be enjoyed if you do. If you don't, try to find a common thread of interest and magnify that. I have a friend who is a dedicated vegetarian. Her husband's parents are dedicated hunters. My friend cannot stand the thought of hunting deer, rabbits and ducks. That was all her husband's parents talked about when they visited. She felt like never going back to see them. Finally, during one visit, she confessed that it actually made her feel physically sick to hear them talk about hunting. She asked their help to find other areas that they might have in common. Through this process, the three of them learned that they all had a passion for poetry. From then on, they shared poetry together, and the subject

of hunting was never discussed again. The mother even began learning how to make vegetarian dishes so her daughter-in-law would feel more comfortable.

4. Listen to his parents and find out about their lives. Everyone loves to be heard. I know a powerful woman who is a PhD physicist and has an important job as head instructor at a major university. Her husband's parents are simple people with only a high school education. They felt intimidated around her and would just sit quietly. She felt badly that, when she would talk about her job and students, they never really seemed to listen. Finally, she tried just asking them simple questions to bring them out. She wanted to know all about her husband and what he was like at each stage of his growing up. The parents lit up and enthusiastically told her every detail they could remember.

Then, she learned that they were good gardeners. She knew nothing about gardening and asked them to teach her what they knew. That became the basis of a relationship that was able to go on for years. She learned valuable advice about gardening from them, and they no longer felt intimidated by her. She realized that, by listening, she was able to bond with them. There were plenty of people who listened to her each day and, in this one relationship, it served her well to just be the listener.

More on Boundaries

It is important to say no when something doesn't feel right. Barry's parents used to plan visits that lasted two weeks, staying in one of our daughters' bedrooms. By the end of that time, all of us were irritable with each other. Barry's dad missed the privacy of his own home and watching the ball game on TV. We did not have a TV. Barry and I missed our privacy and soon became irritable with each other. The children sensed our tension and began fighting more. Only Barry's mother loved the long visits and would have liked them to be even longer.

I finally had to say no to the two-week visits and asked for just one week. Even that was too long. Finally we agreed on four-day visits. They drove up from San Diego and spent four days with us over Thanksgiving and also in the summer. And we visited with them in San Diego for four days. This worked much better. Barry's mom still would have preferred a longer visit, but it was important to me that we all enjoy the time together rather than being irritable with each other. Barry's dad probably would have preferred a shorter visit. So it was a compromise that started with being able to say no.

If it can be avoided, try not to borrow money from your partner's parents. This is a tricky thing. On one hand it seems convenient. They might have more money than you do and may be willing to loan the money. But this sets up a potentially harmful situation in your relationship with them. As long as you owe them money, it puts them more in the role of a parent and you as the children. It's easy for you to lose your power in this situation.

One time we decided to borrow money from Barry's parents. Fresh out of medical school and owing more money than we had, we had no money when our only vehicle needed a new engine. We asked to borrow the money and they sent it immediately. But then we noticed a subtle change in our relationship with them. They started giving us more unsolicited advice, and being a little more critical of our lifestyle choices. As soon as we could, we paid back the money, and noticed a positive change in our relationship with them. Sometimes, borrowing money from your partner's parents cannot be avoided, but an honest effort to repay that money is always good for the relationship.

Remember to be thoughtful of his parents.

Some men are good at remembering birthdays and Mother's and Father's Days. Some men are not so good at this kind of remembering. Barry falls into the latter group. When we were first married, I always remembered my parents' birthdays and other special occasions. I figured that I would take care of my parents and he would take care of his parents. That seemed reasonable. Well it didn't work, and time and again Barry's parents were forgotten.

Reminding Barry helped a bit, but didn't solve the problem. Year after year, Barry's mother was hurt on

Mother's Day. Finally, I bought the cards along with the ones for my parents. I would put them on the table, write something myself and then ask Barry to simply write in each one. When given the opportunity so clearly, he would then write touching things for both of our parents. I addressed them and sent them off. Now this may be a little codependent, but it worked, and Barry's parents enjoyed being included in the thoughtfulness. Barry is thoughtful in other ways, but sending out cards is just not his strength.

Above all else, tell his parents how much you love their son. This may be the single most powerful thing you can do with his parents.

> *I feel really loved by Suzanne when she reaches out and sincerely accepts all my family and friends, in spite of who they might be, just because they're my family and friends.*
> –Aaron Nitzkin, Davis, CA

Love Him in Public Too

It's not enough to love your man when it's just the two of you. Don't ever hesitate to show your love in public as well.

Okay, it doesn't need to be overdone when you're in public. If he's an introvert, you might embarrass him by gushing too much around other people. Just be sensitive to how he feels, just as much as how you feel.

So how can you love him in public? Again, be sensitive to his feelings just as much as to your own. Reach out and take his hand because he likes it. If you take his hand because you like it, it may come across as sweet, but it is not necessarily demonstrating your love for him.

How about if you're an extrovert and he's an introvert? When with friends, put your arm around your man while talking with other people, especially another man. Give a clear signal to everyone about who you're with and who you love. Do this especially if he feels nervous or insecure, or you're with your friends rather than his friends.

Don't make the mistake of ignoring your man in public, in the name of being independent or fearing codependence. Something else may be at play. Another man giving you attention may be flattering to your ego. You might think, "What harm could a little innocent flirting do?" First of all, flirting is never innocent or harmless. Flirting is an exchange of sexual energy. It is degrading to your man, and gives a clear message that you are not committed to him.

Sometimes, women will say to us, "He's too jealous and insecure!" In other words, he has the problem. Or: "I'm not having sex with other men! Why does he get all bent out of shape?" You may feel you're having an innocent conversation with another man but, if your man feels hurt or abandoned, pay close attention. You may have something important to learn from him. If you feel it is hampering your style, or obstructing your freedom, to include your man or put your arm around him, then you have a problem! It is also your problem if you feel that including your man might somehow upset the other man. You may have a fear of commitment, or a fear of attachment.

Love him by including him in your conversations. If he's deeply involved in his own conversation, don't drag him away. But if he's standing by himself, you love him by bringing him into your conversation.

Many men feel especially loved through touch. If this is true of your man, don't miss any opportunity to touch him. He may often reach out to hold your hand in public but, when you reach out for his hand first, you clearly love him. He may often hold you or hug you in public, because this is how he says to you, "I love you." Even if you completely enjoy his touch, sometimes hold him or hug him first, and he will feel your love.

Joyce and I have a private joke. She will sometimes ask me how she can love me more. It's sweet and sincere. My standard answer: "Just touch me more!" Joyce laughs and then asks, "Is that all? Isn't there some other way?" I pretend to be in deep thought for a minute and finally say, "Hmmmm, maybe you're right. Let me think ... No."

Don't get me wrong. I feel loved by Joyce in a multitude of ways. For example, in public, I feel loved by the many ways she looks at me with love and support for who I am, as well as looking to me for support or encouragement. Whether in social situations or leading a workshop, she has a way of glancing at me when she speaks, that shows me how important I am to her. And when I speak, I feel her attention and gaze upon me. She listens deeply to me, and I feel loved by this.

Love your man by experimenting with different ways of public shows of love and affection. Joyce and I are often in airports. We watch lovers being reunited after a flight. They throw themselves into each other's arms. Even though we travel together, we had the idea of pretending that only one of us had been traveling. Arriving in baggage claim, a common area of greeting, Joyce sometimes calls out to me, "Sweetie, how was your flight?" And then we fall into a lover's embrace, not ashamed to hold one another close and even passionately kiss as lovers who have been separated. It's something that is completely sanctioned in baggage claim. Even if it was not, people look at these two passionate seniors and think it's adorable!

To Really Become Vulnerable with a Man

TO BE VULNERABLE WITH YOUR MAN IS TO ALLOW YOUR-SELF TO BE SEEN AND KNOWN IN YOUR ENTIRETY, not just your powerful, independent, secure, loving and capable self. To be vulnerable is to show him your fear, pain, shame, and need for love. To be vulnerable, contrary to what many people think, makes you truly attractive, even irresistible.

The opposite of vulnerability is keeping on your armor, your protection from being hurt. Trouble is, this armor also keeps love away from you.

Joyce has been my greatest teacher of vulnerability. When she needs love, which we all do from time to time, she approaches me tenderly and respectfully, and asks, "Barry, can you hold me and let me know everything will be all right?"

It's so simple and direct, so without pretense, so disarming, and so without the pressure or demand for me to do anything. She doesn't launch into an explanation of what's bothering her. She stays with the feeling, and her need for comfort and reassurance. In that moment, there is no powerful and loving woman standing before me … just a little girl who's hurt or scared. It's a direct appeal to all that is father within me. No matter how busy I am in that moment, no matter how much I am in my head, Joyce's pure vulnerability eclipses my mind and opens my heart. I will drop anything to comfort that pure expression of a child's need for love. I put my arms around Joyce and feel her melt against my body. Without even knowing the details of her worries, I am able to reassure her all will be well, no different than I did when our children were small and defenseless, and unable to articulate what was bothering them.

Sometimes I slip and begin to ask her questions before she's ready to speak as an adult. She'll speak with the uncontaminated voice of a child, "Please just keep holding me. I don't feel ready yet to speak." And again she directly appeals to the heart of the father within me. It is a pure joy to be needed and honored so deeply.

Vulnerability-Challenged

Many women have great difficulty with Joyce's example. In the companion to this book, *To Really Love a Woman*, we wrote about a woman, Kaitlyn, who also needs to be included here:

Kaitlyn complained about having to take care of three children, ages four, seven, and thirty-eight. The last one was her husband, Tomas. She wanted him to be more responsible with their two "real" children. When she was too exhausted to put them to bed and she asked Tomas for help, instead of calming them down, he would get them so worked up, it would then take Kaitlyn an extra hour to settle them down. When she left him alone with the kids, she didn't trust him to feed them properly or keep them safe enough. In her own words, "Why does he have to be such a little child? I need him to be a father. I need his help with our children."

Tomas admitted his difficulty taking responsibility, and his tendency to just let Kaitlyn take over with the children's care since she was so much better at it. He also wished Kaitlyn would "lighten up." He described her as too responsible, too serious, too much like his mother.

Joyce and I knew exactly how to proceed with this couple. Kaitlyn didn't only need Tomas to be a better father for their children. She desperately needed him to father her own inner child as well. Tomas, on the other hand, was stuck relating to his wife as a mother figure, and was blind to the little girl needing his love.

We pointed this out to these two and were immediately met with Kaitlyn's resistance. "I'm aware of my inner child, but every time I ask Tomas to be more present with me, he can't do it. How can I trust him to father me when he keeps disappointing me?"

Joyce and I saw that Kaitlyn needed to be more vulnerable, rather than asking Tomas the way a mother would ask a son. He would understandably feel pressured and perhaps defensive. We also saw that Tomas was blind to the little girl inside his wife. If anything, he seemed cowed by the dominant presence of her motherhood.

We asked Kaitlyn to lean her head against Tomas's chest, like a little girl leaning into the strength and love of a compassionate father. Mumbling, "This is never going to work," she reluctantly did as we asked. In her physically vulnerable condition we asked, "Did your father ever hold you like this?"

"Are you kidding? My father needed my love and help much more than I needed his. I was the one taking care of both my parents. They both were alcoholics and pretty much useless as parents."

"Ah," we said, "but every child needs to be taken care of. You're no exception. Can you remember a time in your childhood when you urgently needed your father's care?"

Kaitlyn was quiet for a moment while she thought. "Well, yeah," she finally said. "One evening when I was probably eight years old, I was playing upstairs and my fourteen-year-old cousin came into my room and started getting aggressive with me. He started reaching into my pants. I told him to stop, but he wouldn't. I somehow broke away and ran downstairs because I knew my father was home. I don't remember where my mother was. I found my father passed out on the couch. When I told him I was scared and needed his help, he didn't even open his eyes. He just told me to go away. I had to spend the rest of the evening hiding from my cousin, and yet stay as close as I could near my useless father."

Kaitlyn was crying. In that moment, she looked like a helpless and terrified eight-year-old girl.

We noticed Tomas's hands had started gently caressing Kaitlyn's head the moment she started crying, and asked him what he was feeling.

"I never heard that story. It makes me sad. I wish I could've been there to protect you, Katie."

We seized the opportunity for healing. "Tomas, imagine yourself in that house, walking into Kaitlyn's room and seeing her cousin molesting her. What would you like to say?"

Tomas seemed on fire, "Stop touching her this minute! How dare you take advantage of her like that! Leave this room immediately!"

The power coming through her husband caused something to let go inside Kaitlyn. It was just what she needed. She started sobbing uncontrollably. After a while, she found her voice, "Nobody's ever protected me like that."

"Kaitlyn," we urged, "open your eyes and look at Tomas."

She did.

"Can you clearly see a father who is able to take care of you ... even protect you?"

"I never knew this part of you, Tomas," she meekly admitted. "I like it."

"And Tomas, can you clearly see that eight-year-old girl hiding near her father, still needing love and safety?"

Tomas smiled warmly with moist eyes looking down upon his wife/daughter's head against his chest, "Katie, I think I've never seen you so beautiful, so real … so vulnerable."

In that moment, both were beaming through their tears.

"Tomas and Kaitlyn," we began, "this is a key to your happiness as a couple. Positioning yourselves as often as possible just like this as a nurturing father and little girl can be one of the most powerful practices you could ever do together. The father in you, Tomas, has been dormant, and the little girl who needs safety in you, Kaitlyn, has also been in hiding, just like you had to do that night so long ago. Express these two parts of yourselves, and your marriage will come back into balance, and you will soar together into a much higher love than you ever thought possible."

Too many women think they're being vulnerable when they're really not. Kaitlyn was convinced she was being vulnerable each time she asked Tomas for help. Instead, she was asking the way a mother would ask a child, and Tomas reacted accordingly. It wasn't even her choice of words. They were the right words. It was a slight edge to the tone of her voice, imperceptible to her, and not consciously perceptible to him. It was the voice of a mother, not a child. Tomas didn't understand why his heart clamped shut, and he felt like running away. Nobody likes being treated as a child. But her true vulnerability in our office opened Tomas's heart just like Joyce's true vulnerability opens my heart.

Practice

> Identify and feel the little child part of you. Yes, there is the little child who wants to play, sing or dance, but for this exercise focus on the aspect of the little child that needs to be fathered. What does this mean? Perhaps it's the feeling of being held safely, or being told you're special, or being validated and accepted for what you think and feel.
>
> When you are ready, ask your partner with the voice of a child, rather than demand as a parent, to be held as a little child. And especially, let him know specifically what that little child needs.
>
> Some examples:
>
> "I'm scared. Please tell me I'm safe in your arms."
>
> "My father was gone from home so much of the time. Was it my fault? Do I deserve the love of a father?"

"I felt so criticized by my dad for my feelings and sensitivity growing up. Is there something wrong with me?"

Look more deeply at your partner. See if you can notice his loving father self, just waiting to be needed by you. If you are stuck seeing him as a little boy, just look deeper. The father may be partly hidden, but it's there, if you just look deeper. It matters not whether he actually has children. Every man is still a father.

If he reaches out to hold you, if he lights up with a smile, if he speaks words of love or reassurance, you have succeeded. You have been truly vulnerable. If he doesn't respond in the way you hoped, if he seems to close down or pull away from you, chances are you have not been truly vulnerable.

Okay, there's a small chance you have been vulnerable and it scares him, especially if it takes him by surprise, or he feels hurt by you and is busy protecting himself from further hurt.

There's also the possibility that one of his parents (likely his mother) has needed too much from him, has made him into a kind of surrogate father or lover. This is a form of child abuse.

If you're convinced you're being vulnerable and he still stays away or, worse, belittles you, then you need professional help. A good counselor/therapist should be able to spot and help you work with abusive dynamics in your relationship.

Bottom line, the little girl inside you needs to feel safe. To really love a man is to vulnerably show him this need for safety. You then empower him to protect you.

There is perhaps nothing I like better than to protect the little girl within Joyce. When I do this well, when I create an atmosphere of safety around her, an invisible force field of protection, I can feel the rosebud of her heart blossom in beauty. When she feels safe in my presence, she can let go of her own danger-watch. Instead of going to sleep because I'm on watch, she can wake up to her deeper sensitive feelings, to her love. Joyce loves me by completely receiving this protection.

> *I know I am loved by Adora when I look into her eyes and I see the little girl inside of her surrendering her heart to me.*
> –George Chipman, Santa Cruz, CA

To Really Love the Father in a Man

EVERY MAN IS ALSO A FATHER. It doesn't matter whether he has children or not. To really love a man is to love and acknowledge the father part of him.

I have never met a parent (father or mother) who did not have some amount of insecurity about their parenting performance. If you share children with a man, he is most certainly hungry for any words of acknowledgement that he is doing a good job as a father. Maybe you feel you are the primary caregiver of the children. Maybe he is not as present as you are with the children. Maybe you even disagree with some of his parenting techniques. Still, find something, anything, positive about him as a father, and tell him.

If the children are his and not yours by birth, you may have more objectivity to see the healthy as well as the unhealthy interactions he has with his children. Appreciate his good fathering many times for every one time you need to give him "feedback." And preface the feedback with words something like this: "You're a great father, and there's something I just noticed that didn't feel so good to me. Is this a good time for me to tell you?"

If he's helping you raise your children, and has no children of his own, find ways to appreciate his supportive fathering energy. This will mean so much to him. Fathers often feel peripheral to the often stronger bond between mother and children. Add to this mix the fact that he is a stepfather, and his insecurity jumps up a notch.

If neither of you has children, look for ways that he fathers you and love him by acknowledging this fathering love. As I said before, every man is also a father. Sometimes, this inner father comes out more after he has children. Sometimes this father instinct kicks in the moment he holds his first child. Joyce told me something profound when I held our first-born, Rami, for the first time: "Barry, it feels like something new has been born in you. Seeing you hold our daughter makes me realize there's a whole new part of you for me to love."

Yet, regardless of whether or not he has children, there have been many ways he has been fathering you. I'm talking especially about positive, loving, nurturing fathering, not treating you like a child, scolding you for mistakes, or controlling you in any way.

It's the loving father within a man that best defines him as a father. What is this? And how can you identify this energy? Naturally, it would be good for you to understand how he fathers you, so you can notice it and appreciate him for this fathering.

He fathers you by keeping you safe. He keeps you physically safe by driving carefully, clearing brush from around the house in case of fire, holding your hand in dangerous situations, and many other ways. Love him by appreciating all of these things.

He provides emotional safety by holding you when you are sad, by being honest with you so you can always trust him, and by carefully listening to what you say. Again, love him by appreciating each act of emotional safety.

He fathers you by encouraging you to take risks in your life. Notice when he loves you by challenging you to push past your fears, especially when he takes time to listen to and understand your fears.

He fathers you by honoring your opinion. When you don't feel comfortable with his opinion, and he accepts your point of view and your feelings without putting pressure on you to change, acknowledge the generosity of this fathering.

He fathers you by supporting you in all your endeavors. Thank him for his encouragement.

He fathers you by listening fully to you. Thank him when he gives you his full listening attention.

He fathers you by accepting you as you are, rather than who he wants you to become. Perhaps your birth father did not do this, so it is especially healing when your partner does. Don't miss any opportunity to acknowledge him for this "re-fathering."

What really makes me feel loved is something that Emily said to me before our baby girl, Charlotte, came into our lives: "No matter what, we have to make our relationship the top priority." I had no idea how valuable and exactly correct this sage piece of wisdom was. It has made me feel loved, and cared for, when our attention was naturally going to our newborn baby. Emily has reminded me so many times in her actions and words over the last two years just how important and loved I am. Our commitment of putting our relationship first, while at first glance may sound selfish, is the most unselfish thing we can do to lovingly raise our child and give her an example of what a loving relationship looks like. Knowing and feeling secure in this commitment of love in our relationship allows me to give more love to both Emily and Charlotte. Feeling that I am a priority in my wife's world has helped me get through some dark places that I've experienced over the last two years as I'm trying to figure out my new role as a parent.
–Justin Pohn, Louisville, KY

To Really Receive a Man

> *Humble yourself to receive before you can truly give.*
> Native American saying

TO REALLY LOVE A MAN IS TO RECEIVE FROM HIM – or even better, *to receive him*. Receiving is a high art form. Many of us are taught that it is more blessed to give than to receive. Well, it is blessed to give, but not more blessed than to receive. When you receive from a man you empower him. Too many men are tentative and unsure when it comes to loving. They don't know when an act of love is really love unless they see you receiving it. It may feel good for a man to give his love to you, but he gets a deep sense of validation by your gracious acceptance of what *and how* he gives.

He may give you flowers, which feels good in itself, but when you thank him and smile warmly, he feels ten times better. This is receiving. He may help you in some way – cooking an unexpected dinner, cleaning something that you normally clean, or helping with the children in some way that you don't expect – just because it feels good for him to help. But your sincerely thanking him feels much better to him than the actual giving. He may appreciate something about you – the way you look, your intelligence, your caring nature. He knows the appreciation is an act of love by the way you receive it. Believe me, nothing makes him happier than to light you up.

Yes, he may have a hard time receiving your gratitude or appreciation. Many men as well as women are "receiving-challenged." But it does fulfill him to see you receive from him.

Many women sadly grow up learning that men are selfish and unable to give, that they only take. In the movie *Enchanted*, Amy Adams' character, Giselle, and the little girl start bonding and talking about relationships. The little girl says, "Men only want one thing!"

"What is that?" Giselle innocently asks.

The little girl replies with an exaggerated sigh, "I don't know, no one will tell me!"

Seeing men as selfish can be a self-fulfilling prophecy. If you look hard enough for how men only want something from you, then that is all you will see. But if you sincerely look for how much men want to give to you, if you open to the diversity of his gifts, you will empower him to feel like the greatest lover in the world.

Joyce's receptivity is one of the greatest ways she loves me. She loves me by allowing me to love her. Her receiving is not passive. Instead, her receiving is a graceful act of gratitude, the presentation of a beautiful empty vase which lovingly invites me to pour my love into it.

Joyce loves me by lighting up when I tell her how beautiful she is. Sometimes she asks, "Really?" with the innocence of someone who has no idea how gorgeous she really is. Although a part of her has trouble seeing her beauty, just like a part of me has trouble seeing my own beauty, she nevertheless drinks in my words. It is this receiving that lets me know I am loved.

Joyce receives me by listening carefully when I speak. She wants to hear every word. Sometimes, it takes me longer than her to tell a story. She knows she could tell the same story in a fraction of the time. It's more than patience however. I don't feel loved only by her patience with my speaking. I feel loved when she celebrates my uniqueness – even my quirkiness. I feel loved when she appreciates the way I say things, or the unusual way my mind works.

If she asks me a deeper question, especially one that involves my feelings, she has learned to give me time to access my feelings. She knows it takes longer for me to get to my inner feelings. Men have been described as having to go down into a deep well to identify their feelings. It is a journey that takes time and cannot be rushed. She knows she will stop my process and bring me back up into my head if she asks me another question. I feel so loved by her in her gentle waiting silence.

This next one is not a little thing. Joyce receives me by laughing at the funny things I say or do. Her laughter is so genuine, so free, that it makes me feel wonderfully loved. The deeper her laughter, the more I feel loved. It's so much more than her finding me funny. It's more about the way she can let herself completely go, that I have allowed her to become safe enough to wholeheartedly let down her guard. Okay, I love playing out the fool, the imp, the jokester part of me. But her laughter lets me know she really gets me, really receives all of me.

We used to bring groups, including adults and children, on annual river trips on the Klamath River. For some strange reason, I have been chosen by the guides (our own children among them) to oversee the porta-potty. We can be a fairly large group, camping together in a fragile environment. It takes a certain amount of consciousness and dedication to the environment to effectively contain and dispose of our bodily waste. Of course I try to bring as much humor as possible to the potty orientation, which has the potential of not being a particularly inspiring talk. I sometimes wonder if some of the participants expect powder rooms with flush toilets magically materializing on our beach campsites. Sometimes, I take on the persona of "Swami Patidas," who speaks eloquently about the mystical act of using a porta-potty.

One evening around the campfire, Duncan, a member of the group and a comedian in his own right, got into playing the part of the "Chief," to the great amusement of the children as well as the adults. At one point he was giving everyone their Native American names and he came to me, lowering his voice to a deep rumble, "Barry, I now name you 'Running Potty'!"

Everyone laughed. I sat there for a moment, inwardly trying on my new name. Something about it just didn't feel right to me. When the laughter stopped, I just had to speak up for myself, "Chief?"

"Yes, Running Potty?"

"I'm so sorry to disagree with you, but this name just doesn't feel quite right to me. May I change my name?"

"Certainly, Running Potty. What do you suggest?"

"May I change it to Dancing Potty?"

At that point, our friend Trish exploded with laughter and, when she finally caught her breath, she said, "***That's*** the part you want to change!"

Then Joyce and everyone else lost it, including me. We were rolling on the ground with laughter that was totally out of control. It hadn't even occurred to me that I might want to change the "Potty" part of my name. To this day, Joyce still bursts out laughing when she remembers that evening on the river.

Perhaps part of it is being the center of attention, Okay, more than I'd like to admit, but there is unquestionably for me a feeling of being loved. After all these years, Joyce still is vastly entertained by me.

Joyce also loves to receive my wisdom. I can't tell you how loved I feel when she needs help and she comes immediately to me. She has wonderful and wise women friends, and together they support one another in beautiful ways. Still, her first choice is to come to me. She wouldn't come to me if I pulled out my psychological toolbox and tried to fix her problem. She needs me to listen, to really understand her feelings, to ask her key questions that take her deeper into her feelings rather than into her head and rational thinking. She receives me by listening carefully to everything I say, which makes me want to make my every word count.

Then there's the way Joyce receives me during lovemaking. It is so much more than receiving me physically. She lets all of me enter her ... body, mind, and soul. I feel welcomed into heaven by a divine goddess. Her sexual receptivity starts long before we actually make love. She tells me how much she is looking forward to our lovemaking. I feel her eagerness, her anticipation.

I am amazed at how much women take care of men. It's beautiful. It's nurturing. And Joyce is no exception. Her natural instinct is to take care of me. So, especially during lovemaking, when she takes time to fully receive my love and nurturing, when she basks in the divine presence, letting go of her outwardly giving nature and focusing all her energy on receiving my love ... wow, what a gift that is to me!

I love to place my hand over her heart and ask her to receive my love and blessing. Yes, I give my love to her, but it's hard to describe how much her receiving actually gives to me. It's as if the energy of love is being pulled through my body and out my hand, and that movement of energy is delicious to my soul. When there is love, there is no difference between giving and receiving. There is no giver or receiver. Giving is receiving and receiving is giving.

> *My mate, Annee, the Love of My Life, shows me she loves me in a myriad of ways, yet it's the way she looks at me in our quiet times together that always connects me to my heart and tells me that I am deeply loved. Without any words, it's as if she sees my heart. And in that moment of connection, I am inducted into heart-space and know both of us as eternal beings who must have been together many lifetimes, and whose essence is love itself.*
> – David Martin, Monterey, CA

Practice

Next time you are in the presence of your man (and it doesn't matter what you are doing, whether as mundane as washing the dishes together, or sublime as praying together), practice the art of silently receiving. Every time you inhale, feel if you can also draw into your being a loving gift from your beloved. Notice that this has nothing to do with his current state of consciousness – whether he is actually loving you or not. It is all about you drawing in his love with every breath.

Guaranteed he will feel this on some level, whether consciously or unconsciously. Most times this silent receiving will make him noticeably happier. He probably will feel drawn to you. He may ask you what you are doing. If so, you might want to tell him the truth. He may be delighted.

But whether there is a response from him or not, please trust that you love him very well by the spiritual attitude of receiving.

To Really Listen to a Man

WHEN YOU ASK A MAN A PERSONAL QUESTION, do you sit back and listen to his response without any interruptions? Or do you fill in the waiting period with more questions and other talking? Most of us would right away say that we are like the first type of person or at least we want to be. Oddly enough, most of us are like the second and don't realize it.

Recently, Barry and I were doing an intensive workshop with a small group and they became very close to one another. One of the men in the group was asked a question by one of the women. The question held a deep emotional charge for this man. I watched as he took a deep breath, slowly began to answer the question, and then paused as he was collecting his thoughts. He clearly wasn't finished. A woman asked another question, which she felt would help him. The man became silent and soon others were asking him more questions. Each person felt that the way they phrased the question would be able to help him.

I suggested that everyone just be quiet and let him take all the time he needed to answer the question. The room became totally silent for a period of several minutes.

Gradually, the man began to speak again with many pauses. The longer he spoke without the interruption of more questions, the deeper he got until finally he clearly spoke his deepest truth about the question that was asked.

It is a little more typical of men to need a time of silence to answer a question, especially when feelings are involved. If they are pushed or interrupted they will just be quiet and not answer at all. The silence allows him to go to the bottom of his well and bring up a richness of truth. If the journey down into the well of feelings is interrupted by another question or more talking, he will come back up into his mind and not have access to his feelings.

I remember a time when our son came home from his first day of sixth grade. This was a big change for him because, for the first time, he would have several different teachers rather than one, and would be changing classrooms. I wanted to hear all about it. As soon as he walked in the door, I sat him down to his favorite cookies, fresh out of the oven, and asked how his day went.

As he sat there eating the cookies and thinking about the question, I asked him another question, "Did you like changing classes?"

There was more silence and so I started asking more questions. "Did you like your English teacher? Is the new Spanish teacher nice? When does volleyball season start? Are you going on a class trip this year?"

Each question was met with silence. Finally, he got up and said, "Thanks so much for the cookies, Mama. I think I'll start on my homework. There are just too many questions for me."

I sat there for a while feeling disappointed. I had really wanted to hear about our son's first day of sixth grade. Then I realized I had been the only one talking. Rather than asking a question and just listening to whatever came out of that, I filled in the time with question after question and probably tired him out with all the input.

The next time he came home from school, I asked one question and just sat there and listened. There was silence for a while, even a little uncomfortable for me, but then gradually the answer started coming out and, the more I remained quiet, the more he talked.

A sweet couple from Germany told me about an experiment they started in their relationship. Helga was outgoing and could express herself easily. Her husband, Dieter, was quiet and had difficulty expressing himself. Helga yearned to hear Dieter's feelings and would ask him questions. The more questions she asked, the quieter he became. She was growing frustrated and even began to doubt the relationship.

A therapist suggested they try an experiment. They sat together for twenty minutes each day with a timer. First, Helga talked for five minutes while Dieter listened. This was not unusual. When the five-minute timer went off they switched and Dieter talked. He talked about car repairs he wanted to do and places he wanted to take their two boys. This also was not unusual as he often spoke about these things. For the third five minutes, Helga spoke about her deep desire to know her husband better and to hear his feelings. When the timer went off, it was Dieter's final turn. He sat for a long time in total silence. His wife did not speak at all, but continued to look at him with love.

After four minutes in total silence, Dieter began to speak. He spoke feelings that he had never shared with his wife. When the five-minute timer went off, she gently turned it off and asked him to continue. He spoke for a while more, while she sat in complete silence loving and listening to him. She felt close to him when he told her he was finished. They held each other for a long time. She thanked him and told him she had learned things about him that she never knew before.

Dieter and Helga's relationship changed after that twenty-minute experiment. She realized that her husband indeed had deep feelings. He just needed time and complete silence to bring them out. She also saw that it was she herself that was blocking the communication by asking him question after question without really giving him the space to answer. When he didn't answer right away, she grew frustrated with him, which closed him down altogether. He never realized that he needed time to access feelings. He compared himself to his wife. He thought that perhaps he was flawed in some way and unable to reach his deep feelings. Sometimes he wished his wife would stop asking questions, but he felt it would hurt her to ask her to stop.

I have recommended this experiment to couples and, without exception, there have been positive results. If ever a woman says to me, "My husband will not share his feelings with me," then I ask her to try this experiment.

As your own experiment, try asking your man a question. Sometimes it helps to get his attention first with something like, "Is this a good time to ask you something?" If his answer is yes, go ahead and ask your question. Then just sit back and listen, allowing him to take all the time he needs to answer. There might be a long silence or pauses, but rather than fill in the spaces with more questions and talking, just be quiet and listen. Even if you are uncomfortable with the silence, just be quiet and listen as a way to love him. If you are patient enough, your man will open up and speak, and this will be a gift to both of you.

Twenty-Minute Listening Exercise

It can be helpful to arrange a special time to do this listening practice. Five minutes per turn is a good suggested starting point. You may find you both want more time, but we suggest each person gets the same amount of time. This keeps a good balance. The rules are simple:

1. Each person speaks for five minutes, and then a second round makes it a total of twenty minutes.

2. Use a timer. The last thing you want to do is keep looking at your watch.

3. Keep it open-ended, but keep in mind the goal of communicating feelings as much as possible.

4. The person listening does just that. Not one word. Even try to keep your facial expressions as attentive and loving as possible, rather than communicating impatience or frustration. Remember, it often takes time for your partner to travel down to the well of feeling and find words to express them.

Barry: I have always loved the song, *"Will You Still Love Me Tomorrow?"* by Carole King. It's on my iPod, which I sometimes listen to on shuffle mode. Recently, while it played, I paid extra attention to the lyrics. I listened to the song from the point of view of the silence a man needs after an important question is asked of him. The song starts out sweetly romantic:

"Tonight you're mine completely.
You give your love so sweetly.
Tonight the light of love is in your eyes..."

Then comes the riveting question:

"But will you love me tomorrow?"

All right, it's a song. The music isn't about to stop to give time to the person to go deeply into feelings and then come up with an answer. But still it's a good illustration of what not to do. The song continues:

"Is this a lasting treasure,
Or just a moment's pleasure?
Can I believe the magic of your sighs?
Will you still love me tomorrow?"

Count them. Three new questions, and then back to the first question. The recipient of this song is probably reeling, unable to answer with heartfelt truth. The song continues:

*"Tonight with words unspoken,
You said that I'm the only one."*

(Sweet, and then comes the "But.")

*"BUT will my heart be broken
When the night meets the morning sun?"*

(Another good place for five minutes of silence but, again, it wouldn't quite work in a song)

*"I'd like to know that your love
Is love I can be sure of.
So tell me now and I won't ask again,
Will you still love me tomorrow?"*

(How about, "I know you can't tell me now because of all these questions.")

Again, I love this song. I'm certainly not trying to criticize it. And, to tell you the truth, it probably couldn't be written any differently. If Carole King had sung the song with the needed long pauses after each question, the song would have bombed.

On a more serious note, at a recent couple's workshop, Joyce and I led the twenty-minute listening exercise for the first time, and did the exercise ourselves. We both had a great experience, and learned something new about each other. (It's so much fun to learn something new after so many years together!) In my second five-minute turn to speak, I had no idea what I would share with Joyce. It took perhaps a full minute of silence before I started talking about writing. Joyce knows I love to write, but she doesn't know why. For the next four minutes I told her why I love to write, that it's a form of meditation for me. There are moments when I feel "in the flow," when the writing is effortless, and I feel so energized that I don't want to stop.

When we finished the practice, Joyce told me she now really understands my love of writing. Just by listening to me without interruption, she felt my deepest feelings about writing. And I felt deeply loved by her listening and understanding.

What really makes me feel loved by Linda are all of the things that she doesn't say. Like when I get lost when we're driving somewhere and she doesn't remind me that she made the suggestion that we take the road that I chose not to take and that was the correct one.

I love how she doesn't give me advice when I'm confused. She doesn't tell me what she thinks I need to do or say or see or understand, but rather she just lets me be where I am, how I am, and she joins me there. Then I'm no longer feeling alone and even though nothing on the outside has changed, on the inside, it all feels different.

She doesn't try to get me unstuck when I am stuck and she doesn't finish my sentences when I can't find the right words. She just hangs in there with me giving me the patience and compassion in her presence that I lack in my own at those times.

– Charlie Bloom, Santa Cruz, CA

Using Our Words Wisely

AN IMPORTANT WAY TO LOVE A MAN IS TO USE YOUR WORDS WISELY. I, like many women, like to process my feelings out loud. I like to look at things from many different angles as I talk about them. For Barry and for a lot of men, they do not like to talk over feelings as much as women. Most men talk about other things that don't necessarily interest women all that much, such as sports, projects, trips, or other action-oriented topics.

At the moment, we are completing an eight-day writing retreat at a beautiful cottage in Hawaii, a gift from some friends. Even though the ocean scenery and the jungle trails have called to us deeply, we have stayed inside writing except for a few hours a day. Complicating this retreat, there was also a major family crisis involving our daughter. Her husband suddenly left her and did not want to work on the relationship anymore. This came as a complete shock to Rami, to their little two-year-old son as well as both of us.

Barry and I were sad about this situation and talked about it a lot. The only way we could help was to listen to Rami and love her. I could have talked about it a lot more than Barry, but I needed to be sensitive to his limits, knowing that in several hours or even the next day he would be willing to talk about it again.

When Barry and I go out walking, sit to have a meal, or lie together in bed after a nap, I could fill the time with talking about the crisis back home. And yet I don't. It's not Barry's way to talk things over and over again. Yes, he will listen every day, but he has his limits, and I need to be sensitive to those. He will also hold me when I feel sad about it. I find that if I talk about this situation just the right amount of time for him, he will be totally engaged with me or even share his pain around it as well. If I talk about it too much, he will begin to not listen so carefully.

So every day, we talk about the crisis and, every day, we also have periods of time when we don't. During these times, we talk about our writing, our love for each other, our gratitude for our three children and also our little grandson. When we go out walking along the Hawaiian coast, we are mostly in silence just enjoying the beauty of nature.

I find that Barry's lesser interest in talking about feelings works well for me. I could talk endlessly about something that is upsetting me, but then I don't feel good afterwards. I have put too much attention upon it. Giving Barry a break also gives me a space for inner reflection and a chance to take my problems to God. So I practice restraint because I love Barry, but it also helps me a lot.

I know a woman who talks constantly. When I am with her, even if I am having a hard time myself, she will talk about her life and her feelings almost the entire time. I have seen her do the same thing with her husband. He is a quiet man. When he has a vacation from work, he wants to spend it totally alone. Sometimes he goes on a meditation retreat or else a backpacking trip in the wilderness. Though he loves his wife very much, she is seldom invited on his vacations. Perhaps if she gave him more space to be silent in their relationship, he would not feel that he needed to go off so much by himself.

Barry's ideal vacation is going on a river trip. I enjoy these vacations as well, but certainly not as much as Barry. I sit in the front of the raft, Barry sits in the back guiding and rowing. Barry would be content sitting quietly for hours, studying the river, admiring the natural surroundings, and watching for wildlife. I love looking at the beautiful scenery as we float by but, in all truth, sometimes I feel a bit bored, and I hardly ever feel bored in my life. I would love to just talk and talk about all sorts of things. He sometimes talks with me in the quiet pools between rapids, and I love that. Even though I would love much more conversation, I love Barry by honoring his need for silence.

We used to do river rafting workshops with 15-25 participants while a commercial company would supply the equipment, guides and food. My dear friend Trish came on every trip with us, and we always sat together in the boat. We would talk and talk and, if there were more women on the boat, the conversations got even livelier. Sometimes, Trish and I would float through the calm stretches in our lifejackets. We would become so engrossed in our conversation that we would not notice an approaching rapid until Barry yelled for us to get back in the raft.

On our own two person trips, Barry likes to talk with me around the campfires in the evening, but not so much while on the river. Yes, he will always talk with me if I really need it, but his preference is to be silent and one with the river. So I bring along a little book of inspirations, which I keep in a zip-lock bag. On calm stretches I bring out my little book to read and say a prayer of gratitude. Barry's need for silence has forced me to be more reflective myself and reach inside for an inner conversation.

Find Out What He Really Wants and Needs

YOU MAY THINK THE MAN YOU LOVE IS COMPLETELY UP FRONT WITH WHAT HE WANTS AND NEEDS FROM YOU. Sorry to burst your bubble, but he is most often not. First of all, he often doesn't know what he wants and needs. Or he may mix up the two, wanting one thing but needing something else.

One common example is sex. How often have I wanted sex with Joyce, but really needed acceptance or comfort. Joyce loves me by gently asking me what I really want and need.

You may recognize that your man is unhappy, or even depressed. You may ask him what he wants or needs and he responds with "I don't know." It takes loving patience to sit in front of him and give him permission to feel what he needs. He may not have ever gotten this permission from his parents, or worse, he may have been told what he wants and needs by them. His own wants and needs may have been ignored, rejected or even ridiculed.

Dad: "You want art lessons? Art is for sissies! I don't want anyone calling my son a sissy!"

Mom: "You need me to hold you? I don't have time for that. Besides, you're not a baby anymore."

So you can see, telling your man what he wants or needs is not a good idea. However, gently asking can be quite helpful.

Sometimes it's hard for me to identify what I need. A little while ago, I was on a difficult phone call with someone who was angry and blaming me. Even though it was obvious to me that she was much angrier with her father and her husband (I knew some of the details), she kept projecting it onto me. I apologized for my part and invited her to go deeper, but she refused.

I got off that phone call feeling shaken and walked through the house to the kitchen. Joyce was standing near the entrance to the kitchen. She took one look at me and knew something was wrong. Unbelievably, I walked right past her with hardly a glance, and began busying myself in the kitchen. She could have easily felt brushed off, but instead came quietly up to me and gently asked, "Barry, are you needing love right now?" I closed my eyes for a moment, listened to the "yes" screaming inside me, sheepishly made eye contact with Joyce and admitted my need for her love. She immediately wrapped her arms around me and I melted into her loving embrace.

It can be a huge challenge for a man to recognize and then admit his need for love. For many years, the word "need" to me was a four-letter word as bad as some other bad four-letter words. It implied pathetic weakness. I was so strong, independent, self-sufficient and secure that I didn't need anyone. Like I mentioned previously, it took me having an affair with Joyce's best friend three years after we were married, and Joyce's leaving the marriage, to finally crack open my shell of resistance. I soon discovered that the child inside me was not only still alive and kicking, but also needed Joyce's love. It was rarely safe for me to need love as a child, so I formed a protective shell around that little boy's need for love, and hid it away even from me. The rediscovery of that little boy and his need for love was a cornerstone for a whole new life, and a deeper relationship with my beloved.

Years ago, we heard about a workshop where the facilitator asked everyone to do something different with nametags. Instead of printing their names on them, he asked everyone to print a few words that authentically described who they were. A woman printed on hers, "Child of God." A man scribed, "Divine Lover" on his. But the authenticity (and vulnerability) prize went to one courageous woman who simply printed on her nametag for everyone to read, "I Need Love."

Sharing His Vision

I love Barry by sharing his vision or at least trying it on for size. When we were both twenty-seven years old, we had been married for five years. Up till then, I had financially supported Barry through medical school even while I was in graduate school. Then he did a year of psychiatry residency in Portland, Oregon, while I worked in the department of child psychiatry. I had a great job teaching medical students how to interview children and evaluate them for psychiatric problems. I liked working with the medical students, who were all younger than me, but I really loved being with the children. I felt completely natural with children and, in a short time just by playing with them, a child would open up to me. I felt shy and insecure around people who were older than me.

Toward the end of Barry's first year of residency, the psychiatry program changed from being human-centered to being drug-centered in its approach to patients. One day, Barry came to me and said, "I can't continue with this residency. It goes against who I am. I have a vision of the two of us helping people in a deeper way."

I could understand why he wanted to leave. He only needed one year of residency to get an MD license and this felt like a good vision for him. What I couldn't see was myself joining him. How could I do this work with him when I was afraid of most adults? I gave him my blessing for his vision, but said that I was simply too afraid to join him.

Barry lovingly and gently assured me that his vision definitely included me as well. I knew that only my fear was standing in my way. So I agreed to try his vision on for size. I maintained that if it didn't work for me, I would go back to working with children. Barry was so happy that I was willing to support his vision.

It took nine years to bring that vision, which eventually became my vision as well, into fruition. During those nine years we traveled and studied, had two of our three children, and studied some more while our babies slept. For the past forty years, we have been living the vision that Barry had during his residency. I am so grateful that I pushed past my fear and tried it on for size.

Getting Your Man Out in Nature

Although both men and women need time in nature to restore their souls, there are some men who may need encouragement. Joyce and I have seen too many men who seem to have lost their souls through too little contact with nature. They have lost some vital and earthy part of themselves that comes from connection with nature.

I am writing this piece while sitting next to my tent on a bluff overlooking a stream flowing along a rocky beach and into the Pacific Ocean. I have four days to immerse myself in the wild ruggedness of the Lost Coast in northern California. On my right side is the higher-pitched sound of the stream. In front of me is the deeper roar of the ocean surf. Behind me, I can hear birds singing from the trees and bushes. It's a symphony of natural sounds that feeds my soul as much as my simple backpacking meals feed my body.

I love spending time in nature with Joyce, especially on overnight river trips. The wildness of nature feeds our relationship. The busyness of life falls away as we settle into a rhythm based on the simplest of things: the direction of the wind, a level protected spot to set up our tent, the different moods and sounds of the river, the temperature letting us know how much we need to wear, and the solitude letting us know if we need to wear clothes at all. Nature allows us to see one another in a new and fresher way.

Yet I seem to have a bigger need than Joyce to get away from even our beautiful and private home and land. So perhaps once a year, I make time for a solo retreat away from home. Joyce seems to be able to disconnect from work more easily than I can. She is having her own retreat right now at home. She stays out of the office. Her computer remains off. She even changes the out-going message on our home answering machine to say we are *both* away.

Sometimes, work is more ingrained in a man. Sometimes, our fathers modeled working and earning money as the most important way they loved us. I had this modeled to me by my father. He commuted three hours round-trip by car into New York City to work at a job he didn't enjoy. At the age of fifty, all this abruptly came to an end. While on his way to work one morning, a young man coming from the opposite direction fell asleep while driving and drifted across the highway, crashing head-on into my dad. The young man died. My dad was thrown through the windshield (this was before the days of seat belts and airbags). With a fractured skull, a leg shattered in pieces, and other injuries, he couldn't work for six months, which meant he lost his job.

I write this story about my father because, for him, there was a hidden blessing. While he lay at home recuperating, my mother, on a whim, bought him a beginner's set of oil paints. Not only did he begin painting, but he continued until his death at age seventy-nine. And what did my dad paint most? Nature scenes! Often the ocean that he loved most. His new commute would be to go off into nature to paint. Sometimes, the rest of the family didn't understand his choice of subjects. Once, in the woods, he came across a huge log that he studied and painted for hours. I remember we all made fun of his painting of a log. Last year, while Joyce and I were visiting our brothers' families in Minneapolis, my niece, Jenna, showed us her new apartment. There on the wall in all its glory was "The Log," more beautiful than I had remembered it.

I feel my life was changed for better when, at the age of six, our family moved from Brooklyn to Elmsford, to buy a home in Westchester County north of the city. A tree may indeed grow in Brooklyn, but I didn't see one! To me, Brooklyn was concrete, pavement, apartment buildings, and loud city noises. Westchester, in those days, was woods and farmland, in other words, wilderness compared to Brooklyn. Our backyard was my gateway to a whole new world, a world without pavement and buildings. After school and on weekends, I was an explorer, a pioneer, an adventurer! Just five minutes' walk from my backyard, down in a hollow, was a gigantic (to me) weeping willow. To me it was like the "Hometree" in the movie, *Avatar*. It was a whole world to explore. Split in half by a lightning strike, but still alive, it was my "Hometree." The split made a perfect home or fort where I spent hours by myself, and sometimes with friends, dreaming up adventures.

I have a vivid memory of what I now know was a kind of spiritual initiation ceremony in my preteen years. It involved a long wooden staff and a kind of primitive dance that I invented, inducing me into a trance state. I'm pretty sure this would not have happened in Brooklyn!

Perhaps more so because of these key childhood experiences, my pull to nature is very deep. I used to think I would've made a good park ranger, except I don't think I could have taken the rules and regulations. I'm happier having nature be my recreation rather than my career.

You love your man by encouraging him to get outdoors. More than mowing the lawn (which I love to do!), or pruning the trees (which I also love to do!), encourage him to get away in nature. Especially if he spends most of his time indoors, you give him a great gift by inspiring him to receive from our great earth mother. Go with him sometimes and enjoy nature together, but also allow him to experience solitude in the great outdoors, where he can reclaim his inner pioneer or explorer.

You fill up my senses
Like a night in the forest
Like the mountains in springtime
Like a walk in the rain
Like a storm in the desert
Like a sleepy blue ocean
You fill up my senses
Come fill me again.
– John Denver, *"Annie's Song"*

Going on Adventures with Barry

A way I love Barry is to go on outdoor adventures with him. Now you may be thinking that is not such a big deal. Don't all women love adventures? Well, you just don't realize what adventure means to Barry! Let me give some examples.

Barry is an avid canoeist. His first choice would be to pack up our old and battered seventeen-foot canoe with enough supplies for a week and head down the river into the wilderness. When I go with him, I sit in the front and let him do all of the steering. I am generally happy to just sit and paddle.

Our first camping river trip with the canoe was down the lower section of the Eel River in Northern California. This was to be a short two-day trip. We got to the river late and by the time we were on the river it was getting dark and even darker when we found a suitable camping place. This challenged my security needs just a bit.

The next day was beautiful, sunny and calm, that is until noon when high winds picked up and blew so much sand in our faces that it was impossible to stop to rest on the beaches. We paddled all day fighting the up-river wind. The next and last day the winds picked up so strongly that we had to walk in the shallows close to shore, pulling the canoe or else we would be paddling forward but going backward.

I kept looking at Barry. He was ecstatic! Nothing could stop him from enjoying this time in the wilderness. I know that my going on that trip with him made him very happy. And that was one of our easier trips!

The most memorable was when I finally, after perhaps four years of stalling, agreed to go on the upper portion of the Main Eel River. This was a totally different section from the first, and Barry assured me that this would be a different experience than the first with more current to move us along in case of wind. He kept telling me that it was going to be really relaxing and that in the late afternoon I could lounge in the tent reading my book, which I love to do after a day of paddling, and he would make a fire and heat up the dinner.

Well, he was right about it being different, and he was right that he would build a fire at night to cook dinner. That was all he was right about, however. It was the farthest from relaxing that I have ever experienced. Barry didn't realize that the river was too low. We had missed the right river level by perhaps two days.

We took off for five days of canoeing, only to discover halfway into the first day that the river was too low for our canoe and supplies. There was no way to turn around, however, as there was not a road access for fifty-five miles. Nothing deters Barry's enthusiasm for an adventure and this fact was only mildly disappointing to him. I could have put up a royal complaint, but I came on this trip as an act of love for my adventure-loving husband and I needed to figure out a way to enjoy this.

Because the river was so low, it necessitated that we walk most of the rapids, which were either too shallow and rocky or too high a class level through narrow constrictions in the river. We ended up walking perhaps half of the way down the river. Barry walked in the shallows pulling the canoe and supplies while I walked along the riverbank picking my way over boulders and slippery rocks.

All this would have been tolerable except that, ever since I broke my leg and ankle, I have had a fear of falling and am very careful where I walk. Because we were walking so much of the way, we needed to keep going until it was too dark to see and then be on the river again by first light. This meant over thirteen hours of walking over rocks with an occasional short ride through a calm pool. Barry smiled the whole way because, after all, this was wilderness and a new adventure.

One night I started to get worried. What if something happens to us? After all, we were the only ones on the river. We never saw one other person. It was then that Barry told me that the guidebook warned people to be extremely careful going up into the hills for help, as there are marijuana growers who "... may do to you what they have done to the once plentiful deer who have munched on their frilly leaves."

With his calm reassurance he told me not to worry. Indeed, he is a keen outdoorsman. Thus the days went on in this fashion. There were a few times when it was impossible to walk along the river and we had to be in the canoe for certain rapids. Once, Barry kept me in the boat while he walked behind, keeping the canoe slow and steady. When the canoe started moving too fast, I glanced back to see Barry still holding onto the stern but in water over his head. While I screamed for my life, he managed to stop the canoe just before it crashed into a boulder.

Was that trip relaxing? No! Did it push all of my security buttons? Yes! But it also made Barry extremely happy that I went. My way of loving him was just to go and make the best of it. I did not complain, except for the two times when I sincerely felt that I might die. Barry smiled the entire time and told me over and over again that he was so happy that I had come on the trip. Going on these adventures with him is a way that I love him.

In all fairness, I must admit that this stretch of the Main Eel River is now one of our favorite trips. We learn from experience. We catch it in the narrow window when the water level is just right, and we travel by inflatable raft rather than canoe.

Sometimes we do a compromise trip. We pack up the canoe with supplies and head out to an isolated island in the middle of a beautiful lake. We then set up camp and I stay on the island during the day, while Barry explores with the canoe.

In the winter, he agrees to go on my type of vacation. Last year, we spent a week in Hawaii at a friend's beautiful guesthouse. This summer, we might do another of Barry's dream adventures, rafting the Salmon River in Idaho. Even though I am not thrilled, I know that I will go, because this is such a powerful way to love him. And yes, I am quite sure it will be a memorable adventure.

Apologizing to a Man

TO REALLY LOVE A MAN IS TO APOLOGIZE TO HIM WHEN YOU HURT HIM … whether intentionally or not. You may sometimes be so focused on the ways he hurts you that you miss the pain you cause him.

Joyce and I sometimes tell the following humbling story in our workshops to illustrate mutual responsibility:

Some years back, Joyce and I traveled by plane to lead a workshop on living from the heart on the East Coast. It was Saturday morning and we had about an hour before our host would be driving us to the workshop. We love to go for walks, and so we left for a nearby park. We found a trail wide enough for us to walk side by side. Walking is special to us. It is not only spiritually and physically satisfying, but it can also be a good time to plan. Planning is sometimes difficult for us sitting still. There is something about keeping the energy moving.

On this particular walk, we definitely needed to plan how to begin the workshop, but we began the walk in silence. After some time, Joyce began talking about something challenging that had just happened involving her family. There was another moment of silence, during which Joyce started welling up with a deep sadness arising from her childhood. Meanwhile, in that moment of silence, I noticed something shiny on the path in the woods. I stopped, bent down and picked it up. Wiping the dirt off, I saw that it was a pen, and not an expensive one at that. It was just an ordinary, but shiny, pen. I slipped it into my pocket. I thought I might as well keep it, having just taken the time and energy to pick it up and clean it off.

Joyce did not know I had momentarily stopped, and began speaking, choked with emotion. She turned to look at me, but I was not there. Initially shocked, she turned back and saw me a few steps behind, cleaning off the pen. She felt hurt and abandoned, and let me know these feelings as soon as I caught up to her. Now it was my turn to be shocked, and I jumped into defensive mode, explaining what I was doing. Within perhaps a minute, we had both escalated into anger and blame.

"You abandoned me when I really needed you!!"

"You're attacking me for picking up a pen!!"

We arrived back at our host's house unable to look at one another, and definitely unable to speak to one another. We had just enough time to grab what we needed for the workshop and get into our host's car. Joyce jumped into the empty back seat and I got into the front passenger seat. As our host backed down his driveway, he suddenly stopped the car. I was afraid he was about to confront us about the bad energy we most certainly were emitting. Instead, and I can hardly believe this actually happened, he pointed out the front windshield and commented, "There's a pen on the driveway. Do either of you need a pen?"

"NO," we both screamed in unison, I think actually scaring our host.

Arriving at the workshop a few minutes late, we hurried inside, both of us still fuming and emotionally shut down. There is perhaps no more difficult situation than showing up to be models of a loving relationship and feeling the opposite. But desperate times call for desperate measures. We quickly had everyone find a partner and told them to begin sharing what they wanted and needed from this workshop. Then Joyce and I sat together, feeling the immense pressure to work through our feelings as quickly as possible so we could lead the workshop.

It didn't go well at first. Neither of us could shake the anger. In my peripheral vision, I was aware of the workshop participants who quickly finished the exercise and kept glancing over at us. I prayed that they didn't notice the daggers coming out of our eyes toward each other.

We were entrenched in our own positions of being hurt by the other. Yet we knew our only hope lay in taking responsibility for what each one of us did to equally contribute to the crisis. There was simply no other way we were going to get out of this.

Joyce was convinced my actions were more at fault. If I had been more sensitive to Joyce's emotions, I wouldn't have stopped even to pick up a diamond ring. Or perhaps, I would have said, "Excuse me, Joyce, there appears to be a diamond ring on the ground. Do you mind if I check it out?"

I just couldn't apologize, even with all the pressure. I felt hurt as well. But I couldn't clearly verbalize this, except to say that I felt too hastily and severely judged for an action that felt somehow innocent.

The minutes ticked by. The glances from the group seemed more and more concerned. Joyce and I were sweating from the discomfort and tension, though it was actually cool in the room.

At last, we found the missing pieces to a difficult puzzle. We both realized Joyce's responsibility. She assumed I was aware of her difficult state of feelings, but I was not. It was like a light bulb illuminated in both of us. She took both of my hands and spoke, "Barry, I apologize for not getting your attention before speaking something so vulnerable. It's my responsibility to make sure you're ready and willing to receive me."

My heart felt like leaping. "Thank you so much, Sweetie! I need to apologize, too. I could have been more sensitive to your feelings. I see how you could feel abandoned by my suddenly stopping to pick up something without first communicating with you."

The moment we both took responsibility for our own parts of the conflict, the storm was over. Smiles popped up on both of our faces. Love crept back into our hearts. We held each other in an embrace of gratitude.

But now what about the group? We called everyone together, and told the whole story with humility and vulnerability. Questions and comments came fast and furious. At one point I suggested moving on, but person after person let us know quite clearly that this experience, the conflict, all the feelings, and the resolution through each of us taking responsibility, this was why they were there. This was what they needed most from the workshop. One woman, speaking through her tears, said, "My childhood was filled with tense moments of conflict between my parents. Never once did I see any true resolution. Thank you both for this most wonderful gift!" A man said, "This is the best role-modeling I have ever seen in my life. I've gotten my money's worth out of the workshop in less than an hour. I can go home now." Everyone laughed.

For a relationship to be healthy, both partners need to be willing to take responsibility for their own part in an argument. This can be difficult to do. It is always easier to see your partner's fault than your own. If you're angry or defensive in a situation, look deeper and you will find your own part.

If you take responsibility for your own issues, rather than blaming your partner, you become a powerful person. Insist upon your innocence when you are in conflict with a loved one, and you become weak. Insist upon your victimhood and you become even weaker.

In almost every couple's workshop, we ask the couples to take full responsibility for the pain they have caused their partner by their actions, words, or lack of actions. It is always easier to see the pain your partner has caused you. This is very different. It requires maturity and strength to look at the careless things you have done or said to your mate. We used to have each person ask for forgiveness from their partner, but then realized this is not quite as powerful. Rather than depending upon your partner to forgive you, it is more powerful to acknowledge the ways you have hurt them. It is the same basic principle of "making amends" in the twelve-step programs. Apologizing is proactive. It is directly taking responsibility for the pain you have caused. A sincere apology from the heart helps you and your partner. It is the act of apology that helps, more than your partner's response, acceptance, or forgiveness.

Taking responsibility is not about blaming yourself or labeling yourself a bad person. It is vital to remember that you are not the mistake you made. You are not the careless thing you did. There is a big difference between "regular" shame and "toxic" shame. You can feel shame about making a mistake, but if you identify with the mistake, if you see yourself as the mistake, this becomes toxic shame, which make apology next to impossible. You take responsibility best by seeing yourself as a good person who has made a mistake. In fact, you are a beautiful divine being having a human experience. Knowing this truth, it becomes easy to take responsibility for any mistake – and admit it.

Taking Responsibility

The practice has two parts:

1. First contemplate what you consider to be the biggest ways you have caused pain for your partner. Take responsibility completely. It doesn't work to say, "I did this because you did that." Lead with "I apologize for _____." Or "Even though I never meant to hurt you, I see that I hurt you by _____."

If you are the one listening to your partner's apology, express your gratitude, even if it's not the best apology, or the one you most need.

2. Because your apology may not be the one most needed by your partner, step two involves asking their help: "Is there an apology that you still need from me?" Maybe you have already apologized for something, even years ago, but your partner would love to hear it again. A second apology can take it deeper.

> If you are the one being asked this question, please be sensitive. This is not the time to express your anger. This is the time to be vulnerable and gentle. You might say something like, "I trust that you never meant to hurt me by _____, but it did hurt and I still would love to hear your apology, and that you understand how it hurt."

It is not uncommon during this exercise for a couple to call one of us over to them for help. Typically, the man has apologized with some degree of success, for he probably has heard many times which things he does that hurt her. Then, they have gotten stuck when it's the woman's turn to apologize. She will often say, "I just don't know how I've hurt him. He never lets me know." And he won't be of much help to her, often saying, "I can't remember how she's hurt me. I guess I don't pay attention to those things."

So we stay for a while, stimulating his memory and her sense of responsibility, and before long some important items come to the surface. Here are some of the things we have heard that have hurt him: her condescending tone of voice; her enthusiasm for the children and lack of enthusiasm for him; her criticism; her bossiness; and her lack of affection.

Yes, it is *his* responsibility to speak up when he feels these things. Otherwise, how can she possibly learn to be aware of them. Still, her apologies feel good to him.

And then there are covert ways she has hurt him, of which neither of them is aware. Some examples: seeing his lack of commitment to her rather than looking at her own lack of commitment to herself. We hear this quite a bit. "I'm committed to him, but he's not committed to me." What we often see: true, he's more committed to himself than to her, *but she's also more committed to him than to herself*. It is a disservice to him to give him more of a commitment than she gives to herself. To really love a man is to be equally committed to yourself *and* to him.

How else does a woman hurt a man in less than obvious ways? A woman hurts herself and her man by making his feelings or needs more important than her own. She makes herself smaller and less important when she makes him bigger and more important. She loves to give to him, but it hurts them both when she gives at her own expense. To really love a man is to honor your own feelings and needs as much as his.

A woman creates suffering by not saying "no" enough. When we spent a summer with the Sufis in France, one of the main teachings was to say no to everything in life that does not serve us. It is in being able to say no that a yes can then have more power. A woman hurts herself and her man when she ignores herself and gives in to him, when she wants to say no but lets herself be talked into something. You love a man when you stand your ground and say no. But you really love a man when you say no with as much love as you would say yes, because you know you respect yourself as much as you respect him.

To Resolve Conflict with a Man

IN OUR COUNSELING SESSIONS AND WORKSHOPS, many people share that anger is the hardest part of their relationship and often ask us for constructive ways to resolve conflict.

Conflict happens. We may wish we could get to a point in our relationships where we didn't need to ever argue but, as long as we have egos, we are immersed in the human condition, along with the attachment to our own ideas and desires. And that results in fear, hurt and anger. Yet conflict does not have to be such a horrible thing. In fact, we are blessed when we open to the lessons conflict has to teach us, like more acceptance of all our human feelings.

That said, it's important in loving a man to remember that men, more than women, are often subjected to anger expressed physically as violence. When we were angry as boys, we were typically violent with another boy, or we were hit or beaten ourselves. Physical violence makes a lasting impression. Boys grow into men who quite commonly are afraid of expressing anger because of the fear of violence. Joyce and I typically hear from men, "If I lose control of my anger, it will escalate into violence." Or, "My anger will end up hurting someone or myself."

More so, it is the control of anger that causes the most damage. You may feel blindsided by the energy of his hidden anger, and it hurts even more because it doesn't match his words or actions. Yet anger itself can be expressed without hurting anyone.

It's important to understand the nature of anger, as well as its purpose and usefulness. Most often, anger is a way we protect ourselves from the rawness of pain or fear — feelings that can become unbearable to our fragile and naked psyches. It is also a way we stand up for ourselves, rather than letting ourselves be controlled by another.

Irritation vs Anger

We also need to distinguish between irritation and anger. There is a big difference between the little annoyances that are inevitable in relating and the more serious anger that arises from deeper issues. If something we do annoys him, we need to ask ourselves how important it is for us to continue this behavior. Perhaps it's something we can let go of for the sake of harmony, and as a way to compromise with our beloved.

Here's an example: typically, I make my morning green smoothie before Joyce makes hers. Since I use fresh ginger and sometimes other unusual ingredients that are distasteful to her (like Swiss Chard leaves freshly picked from our garden outside), she has asked me to rinse out the blender jar after I'm done. If I forget, and leave the jar on the counter, the residue quickly dries and then requires more effort for Joyce to soak and scrub the jar. It's a little thing, but still it can be frustrating for her.

If she just cleaned the jar and didn't say anything to me, it wouldn't be healthy. If she tried to rationalize by thinking, "Oh, Barry was just in a hurry today and forgot to rinse out the blender jar," it may work a few times. But if I continued to leave the dirty jar on the counter, the annoyance would eventually build inside her. These little unspoken annoyances have a way of eventually closing your heart to the person you love. You may rationalize, "I may be losing the battle but winning the war," meaning that love is more important than expressing these trivial complaints. But it doesn't work that way in intimate relationships. Every time you hold in an annoyance, you not only lose the battle, you also lose the war a little at a time. Every unspoken frustration has a way of eroding a little bit of your love.

Thankfully, Joyce usually doesn't hold in annoyances or frustrations. Sometimes she communicates lovingly and effectively, "Barry, I really appreciate every time you rinse out the blender jar for me. *And* (not *but*) today you forgot." Even though the criticism was coming, the appreciation empowers me, allowing me to more easily hear the criticism.

Joyce is not perfect. Sometimes she is not so appreciating and says, "Barry, I need you to remember to rinse out the blender jar. It makes it harder for me in the morning." This, of course, doesn't feel as good to me. I'd rather have the appreciation first. But still, I'd much rather hear the criticism than have her keep it inside. That way, I always know where she stands and what she feels.

In addition to expressing our feelings, we need to be willing to resolve these little frustrations, to see them through to the end, to sincerely apologize when it is clear that one of our actions upset our partner ("Oops, I'm sorry Joyce. I know it makes things easier on you when I rinse out the blender jar."). It is just as important to communicate our own upset at something our partner did or said.

It is always best to have these communications in the moment, rather than waiting for a better time. Otherwise, these little upsets become buried in the soil of our being, and our heart closes a little more. Joyce and I have an ongoing issue with our golden retrievers over their digging in our lawn and gardens. They simply have the primal instinct of hunting. They catch the fresh scent of a gopher and immediately start digging. No matter that it's in the lawn or Joyce's prized rose beds. And they have yet to catch a single gopher! Our goal is to catch a dog in the act of digging in a forbidden spot, and growl at it, giving a clear "no" message. Even if we catch a dog in the act of walking away from the recently dug crater, it's too late. Dogs are so "in the moment" that, in a matter of seconds, it has forgotten about the digging. To reprimand it while it is walking away from the scene of the crime, we are now punishing the dog for walking away from the hole.

While people are not exactly like dogs, the same principle applies. Because I grew up in a loud, Brooklyn Jewish family, where nobody was allowed to finish a complete sentence, I have had the habit of interrupting Joyce while she was talking. This has never been okay with her. She grew up in a family where there was actually a moment of silence in between sentences. In our earlier years together, we might be visiting with friends and I typically would interrupt Joyce and not be aware of it. She would feel hurt, but would feel too embarrassed to say anything in front of our friends, and would become silent but withdraw her love from me. I might be aware of the "daggers" shooting at me from her eyes, but not know why. Sometimes, I would be completely unaware of my actions and Joyce's pain. But I would hear all about my transgressions after we left and were alone together. I have to admit, this was not so helpful to me. I might have no memory of what had happened. I might get defensive, or even angry.

Maybe owning dogs has helped Joyce to be more immediate with me. Do I still occasionally interrupt Joyce? I'm sorry to say that I do. Old habits from childhood can be difficult to change. Does Joyce still wait till later to tell me when I've interrupted her? No. She tells me while I'm interrupting her. If it's a minor interruption, she might say something like, "Barry, please, I wasn't finished," with no anger at all. Super effective!

If I interrupt her in the middle of vulnerable feelings, especially if I'm insensitive or cracking a joke, this falls into the category of a major interruption. Then she may express hurt, anger, or both, even if there are people around. Joyce is committed to speaking up for her feelings, and yes, I actually feel loved by her level of honesty. She even appreciates me for how much I've grown in this area. Because of her in-the-moment honesty, I am so much more sensitive to making sure she is finished speaking before I jump in.

In addition to not speaking up in the moment, if you wait to voice your annoyance until the sixth time your partner does that certain irritating thing, you carry the annoyance of the other five times in your voice, and your partner feels blindsided. Love your man (and yourself) enough to be honest every time in the moment when something is not working in the relationship.

Beneath Anger

When anger reaches a certain level of intensity, we need to understand that deeper issues may be crying out for attention. This higher amplitude of anger usually relates back to hurts older than the relationship, but triggered by the present situation.

Maggie would become furious when her husband, Bill, would ignore her when they were with his friends. Unfortunately, she wouldn't say anything until they were driving home, and then the level of her anger shocked Bill.

In a counseling session, Joyce and I asked Maggie if she was ever ignored as a child. Through her tears, she described time after time of being ignored by her parents when their friends were visiting. She felt invisible and worthless to them at these times. Now she understood what was underneath her anger at Bill, which helped her to speak up more if she was starting to feel ignored. And Bill understood how important it was for him to validate and include Maggie when with his friends.

Anger is not only an attack; it is most often a defense against hurt. It's difficult not to take it personally when our partner gets angry with us. With Joyce, because of my attachment to her, I tend to immediately react to her anger at me as a personal offense. When someone is angry with us, it feels like we are being attacked or blamed, but this is the smoke screen. The anger is actually just a way this person is covering up their hurt or pain. Their anger is a sign that they are hurting. It is essential to remember this.

Joyce has been able at times to reach through my anger at her and hold the hurt part of me. This has helped me to let go of the anger and access the pain underneath. Often, we are not successful at this method in the early stages of anger and get locked into defensiveness, which escalates the anger. But our goal is to eventually provide a safe place for the other's upset feelings.

Any build-up of energy needs to be released, vented or transformed in some way. Anger is no different. Sometimes, it just needs to be expressed as a release of steam, and then we feel better — and can perhaps subsequently access our deeper feelings of hurt or fear. What we must remember, however, is that anger does not need to be directed at our partner to be released. This can be hurtful. Anger can be effectively expressed by ourselves, for example by yelling in a car with the windows closed or beating on pillows. It is important that we not ignore or distract ourselves from this energy. Sometimes, simply expressing anger in self-describing words ("I'm feeling angry right now") is helpful. Other times, it doesn't need to be expressed outwardly. It can be enough to feel (and accept that you feel) angry as another way to accept your humanity. Writing in your journal can be a helpful tool, as can physical exercise or being out in nature.

Ultimately, if we want to grow spiritually, we need to take full responsibility for our own anger and what is behind it. It is up to each one of us to accept and confront the hurt, pain or fear hiding underneath our anger. To maintain an angry stance is self-defeating, because it continues to cloak our deeper, more vulnerable feelings.

To Effectively Argue with a Man

How do we effectively argue with a man? And even more importantly, can the way we argue actually show a man our love and respect? Joyce and I say yes. There is healthy and unhealthy anger. Here is an example of unhealthy anger:

Tammie, in a loud voice: "Phil, you are such a jerk. You did it again. You said you'd be home at six, and it's now seven. You don't care shit about me."

"I'm really sorry, Tammie. The traffic was bad and I wanted…"

"I'm not done, Phil. It's only been one week since the last time you were late. I don't trust your word anymore. You say you're going to do something, and then you don't. Don't I matter to you?"

"Of course you matter. I tried to call but only got your voice mail."

"Always with the excuses! I'm tired of your excuses! You don't mean anything you say! I'm done with this marriage!"

Tammie's expression of anger is unhealthy.

Lana and Cade went through the same scenario and here's how they dealt with it:

"Cade, I feel hurt and angry. You said you'd be home at six, and it's now seven. I felt scared that something might have happened to you."

"I'm really sorry, Lana. The traffic was bad, but that's no excuse. I should've called you."

"I understand your intentions were good. I'm just feeling scared, hurt and angry."

Lana is being healthy with her anger. Why? Because she has made no blanket accusations like Tammie's, "You don't care shit about me. I don't trust your word anymore. You don't mean anything you say." Lana allowed Cade to speak without cutting him off. She didn't make threats like Tammie's, "I'm done with this marriage!" She didn't call him any names. Instead, she kept to "I" statements, letting Cade know how she felt, rather than making him wrong or shaming him.

Ideally, most anger can be headed off by addressing the feelings underneath, which are usually hurt or fear. When these deeper feelings are expressed and acknowledged, there often is no need for anger. For example, it is unavoidable that Joyce and I sometimes say or do something that triggers hurt feelings in the other. Usually this is completely unintentional. Our goal is to say something like, "I trust you didn't mean to hurt me by saying/doing _____, but it did hurt me." I have to admit, Joyce is better at it than I am. When she makes that statement, it helps me enormously. She acknowledges that I didn't mean to hurt her. This is important to me, often preventing me from going to an old shame tape, "I'm a bad boy," or "I can't ever do it right."

If Joyce launches angrily right into "You hurt me," I can quickly regress into those old messages from my childhood. It's as if I hear the words "You're a bad person," rather than, "You hurt me." And if I do go into this "toxic" shame place, I can become entrenched there for a long time, shutting down my heart and vulnerability in the process. So just hearing those simple words "I trust you didn't mean to hurt me," helps me so much. It's like hearing "You're a good person, and something you did or said triggered pain in me." Very different indeed.

Without the "toxic" shame, I can then hear her hurt and immediately apologize, which can quickly bring us back to love. If I'm entrenched in the toxic shame of feeling like a bad person, there's no way I can ever apologize for my actions. In that toxic shame, I *am* my actions. They are not separate from me. So it feels like I have to apologize for *me*, rather than my actions or words. Without the toxic shame, it's just something I did. I didn't mean to hurt Joyce. I can sincerely apologize and move on.

When the hurt or fear is not consciously felt and expressed, and this may often be the case, anger is the next level. Just to be clear, here are some general guidelines for the healthy expression of anger with a man:

"I" statements are rarely abusive. "I'm angry," rather than "You did _____," or "You are _____."

Angry questions, like "Why did you do _____," just come across as an interrogation. It can make him feel like a helpless, and then defensive, little boy.

Healthy anger is not intimidating or controlling. Even "I" statements can be abusive if you are scaring your man. If you are physically or emotionally dominating him, you are being abusive. This includes not letting him speak or respond and, of course, touching him in inappropriate or aggressive ways.

Healthy anger stays in the present, rather than bringing up unrelated things from the past to fortify your argument. "You came home an hour late without calling. Yesterday you forgot to bring out the garbage, and the day before you left your dirty dishes on the table." Not healthy.

Healthy anger does not generalize: "You're always breaking your commitments." Avoid the words "always" and "never."

Or jump to conclusions: "You don't like this dress because you think I'm ugly!"

Healthy anger does not make threats of any kind. "Break one more commitment and I'm out of here!"

Name calling or swearing … definitely not healthy.

After the anger is expressed in a healthy way, then it's time for both of you to address the hurt or fear underneath the anger. It's time for each of you to take responsibility for your deeper feelings, and apologize for hurting the other. Cade's apology to Lana allowed her to quickly let go of her anger. Lana acknowledging her hurt and fear made it easier for Cade to apologize.

Address the hurt or fear beneath the anger and there will usually be no need to express anger. Prevention is always more effective. But if the hurt or fear remains elusive, you have a conscious choice to express your anger in a healthy way. Follow the above guidelines and you can have an abuse-free interchange.

Specific Rules for Effectively Arguing with a Man

Along with the above general pointers, here are some more specific guidelines when you find yourself in disharmony with a man:

1. Initially, he may not want to talk at all. You may be ready to verbally work things out. He may want and need some time by himself. Give him a reasonable amount of time, even though it may be difficult for you to postpone the expression of your feelings.

2. He may need more time than you to get into his feelings. Each time you ask him another question, he may go back up to his head to "think" of an answer. Give him the time he needs to really check in. (See *To Really Listen to a Man*.) When Joyce is angry, her thoughts speed up and her feelings are right on the surface. When I am angry, my thoughts and feelings feel like molasses. Everything seems to slow down and get gooey and murky. Joyce has learned

to understand this phenomenon, and tries to give me the time I need to process first by myself.

3. Like I said before, aggressive physical contact may be no big deal to you, but to your man it may activate some degree of PTS (Post-Traumatic Stress). Physical abuse is much more common in boys than girls. If you reactivate his PTS, the resolution of your argument may be a long time coming.

4. Again, stay in the present. He may not remember past hurts as well as you do. Bringing up a whole list of past grievances will only put him in defensive mode.

5. Remember the magic phrase: "I trust you didn't mean to hurt me by _____, and it did." Acknowledge that he is a good man who made a mistake. Otherwise he can easily feel that he is the mistake, where he can go into toxic shame and then either shut down or get defensive.

6. And this is most important. As soon as you can, look for and admit to your responsibility in the argument. Admit to your own leaving your heart, rather than what he did to cause you to leave your heart. Your ego needs to be right. Your ego needs to find fault with him. Your ego will effectively keep love away from you. Choose your heart instead. Your heart will give you the courage (remember that "courage" comes from the French word for "heart").

Resolving Arguments

When Joyce and I are angry with each other, we try to stay connected and work it through to the end. We know we are done when we can sincerely hug and kiss one another and even laugh at our behavior. Because of this, the flame of our love and commitment to one another has been allowed to burn brightly. The following story illustrates this:

On a river trip we were leading years ago, Joyce, the kids, and I were looking forward to a special hike up a side stream to a magical waterfall. John-Nuri, five years old at the time, was excited to prove his capability to do this hike. With his sisters just ahead of him, we all set off.

Five minutes into the hike, with the girls and the rest of the group just ahead of us and out of sight, John-Nuri started to get upset at being behind. I *assumed* Joyce heard his complaining and saw his upset: wrong assumption! At that moment, Joyce remembered John-Nuri's life jacket. She felt he would need it upstream at a place where we needed to swim through a deep pool with cliffs on both sides. She asked me to run back and get the life jacket while the two of them waited. She felt afraid to continue without me because of the several stream crossings ahead. John-Nuri was clearly agitated because, in that moment, he couldn't see or hear the others. Joyce did not register this important detail.

I told Joyce it would take too much time to get the life jacket, and also I felt we didn't need it anyway. I felt confident of my ability to swim through the pool with John-Nuri. I neglected to mention John-Nuri's feelings about being behind.

Not knowing how important it was for John-Nuri to catch up, Joyce *assumed* I was just being lazy. The life jacket was important to her. She was thinking about John-Nuri's safety. I was thinking about his happiness. Both of us were trying to be the best parents we could. Both of us were assuming things ("assume," making an "ass" out of "u" and "me").

For Joyce, the situation also brought up another issue. In the past, I had not always been as sensitive as Joyce to John-Nuri's needs. It had been a cause of friction, especially on the river trips, because Joyce felt less physically confident. This kind of "button-pushing" concerning issues from the past is often a cause of arguments rapidly escalating.

With lightning speed, the disagreement escalated into anger, blame, yelling, even name-calling. Joyce left me with John-Nuri while she went back to get the life jacket. I went ahead with him to try to catch up. When Joyce finally did catch up to us both, there was even more anger than before. With the added elements of emotional wounding and the feeling of betrayal, it was the adults who needed a life jacket!

It wasn't until hours later, at our camp for the night, that we were finally ready to sit with each other and try to work things out. The pain of not being in harmony is too much for us to endure for long. It is often that very suffering that urges us to look within and take responsibility for our own part of the argument. So, when we sat with each other, we had both had enough sadness and were both ready to look inside.

For my part, I realized my wrong assumption about Joyce's awareness of John-Nuri's feelings. Joyce realized her wrong assumption about me being lazy. We were able to acknowledge one another as good, caring parents. We could each apologize for our own assumptions and the unkind words that had been spoken in anger.

When we finally smiled and embraced, we heard a loud clapping and cheering from our children and friends in the kitchen area of our campsite. Slightly embarrassed at our lack of privacy on this particular beach, we smiled and hugged even more at the joy of feeling close once again.

Don't Wait Until It's Too Late

A beautiful way to love a man is to help keep the relationship clear of troublesome issues. Women on the whole are more sensitive when something is out of balance or dysfunctional in a relationship. It might be the man who feels this, but the majority of times it is the woman. Men generally feel that an issue can slide, so it is an act of love on the woman's part to seek help for both of them so that there can be healing and clarity.

Recently, I saw a young couple in counseling. I knew them well for they had come to see me occasionally over the past six years. They had three small children and wanted the marriage to work. They had several important unresolved issues, which we would begin to work on in a session, but then I wouldn't see them for a full year or more. Each time I saw them, the issues had grown in magnitude to the point that their relationship was in serious risk of dissolving. I asked them why they didn't come more often than once a year, and do the work to resolve the issues. They replied that they felt they couldn't afford to come more often. I saw them both drive up separately in relatively new cars, and they recently bought a home, so I knew they weren't poor. In a gentle but firm voice, I told them that a divorce lawyer is going to cost them three to four times the hourly rate that I charged, at many more hours. Unless they did the work to resolve these issues, they were headed in that direction. They got the point and have been seeing me on a regular basis, and finally are doing the work to resolve their issues.

Problems in a relationship, whether an intimate relationship, friendship, sibling, or parent/child, do not just go away on their own. Each time an issue or challenge presents itself in a relationship, there is a golden opportunity to heal and grow closer to that person. Ignoring the issue and hoping it will go away is inviting distance and separation.

When Barry and I lead our couple's workshops, we emphasize the importance of resolving issues completely. Do whatever it takes to bring it through to completion and harmony. You will know that you are complete when you can smile about it and even laugh at how childish you both were at the time. If there is still heaviness and you hope that time will take that away, you have not resolved the issue. An unresolved issue will be like a cancer with the potential to spread into other areas of your relationship, eroding the joy, lightness, love and beauty. The next time there is a new issue between you, this old unresolved issue will be right there too. It can get to be like a stew pot of unresolved issues all coming to the front with even the slightest disharmony. An irritation over the phone bill soon also includes, "Why don't you tell me about our finances," or "Why don't you value me," or "Your mother did the same thing to your father," or "Why did you buy that new sports car." You can see how heavy a relationship like that can get to be, carrying around the weight of all those unresolved issues. Imagine carrying a hundred-pound sack and realize how difficult it would be to dance together.

In our many years of being together, there have been three times when we were unable to resolve an issue on our own. We used all the skills that we have and yet it was still unresolved. In those three times, Barry did not really want to go into counseling. I think for a man it can be a pride thing. He should be able to fix the situation without help.

Finally, at my insistence, we sought professional help because there was a blind spot for each of us. The therapist was able to listen to both of us and help us come to a mutual place of resolution. I feel grateful for that help. Most times, we have been able to work things through on our own. Sometimes, we can clear the issue in a matter of a few minutes, sometimes an hour, and sometimes it can take several days. But we still keep working on it until we both understand our own part and responsibility in the issue, rather than simply blaming each other. With our taking responsibility, there is an even deeper connection and perhaps even humor to the situation. In working each issue through to completion, we have been able to retain a beautiful lightness in our relationship that we both cherish.

Sometimes, in our counseling practice, we see couples that have waited too long. The weight of unresolved issues is just too much and the relationship breaks under this burden. This is sad for us, for we sense, underneath the heaviness, a time when there was a beautiful lightness and joy to the relationship.

When issues are handled as soon as they come up, the lightness can flourish in a relationship and lead two people into a lifetime of fulfilling connection and love. We urge you to take each issue seriously and do whatever it takes to bring it to completion, rather than ignoring it. I often think of my mother's words to me about her sixty-year marriage to my dad, "We worked all of our issues out in the first forty years. The last twenty we basked in the supreme joy of that work."

Often, in our couple's workshops, it is the woman who brings the man. Sometimes these men have to be dragged. We have been doing our work long enough that we can easily spot these men. Though they try to appear calm and collected on the outside, inside they want to run out of the room at the first excuse. The woman usually sits beside him feeling nervous, doubting her decision to bring her husband, feeling that perhaps it was better to have the issue than to try and work on it. Almost like clockwork, we know that by the next day, sometime in the morning, he will relax and start to not only like the workshop but actually love it. At some point he gets that, by being vulnerable with each other and working on the relationship, he is going to get a lot more love and attention. It is not at all unusual for the man to end up enjoying the workshop even more than the woman. At the end, it is often the man who thanks the woman for having the insight to realize that the relationship needed some help.

Remembering the Love and Letting the Rest Go

I have been blessed with a really good memory. Perhaps this is genetic because my dad, even at the age of eighty-nine, could remember details from his past, and my brother has an excellent memory as well. Since Barry and I have been together for so many years, there are a lot of memories. A way of loving him is to remember the truly good memories and let go of the memories in which I felt hurt or unfairly treated by him. Since Barry sometimes cannot remember details of memories as well as I can, when we are on a long drive or sitting in the hot tub at night, I enjoy helping him remember beautiful, loving and sometimes funny memories. He enjoys these memories a lot and usually, once we get started, he fills in a few details as well.

Life is constantly giving us opportunities to make choices as to what we remember. Each day holds many different moments – some painful, joyful, confusing, happy, peaceful, angry and loving. We decide which ones to remember. Our memories can't hold all these moments, so the ones we choose to remember are important, for we will learn and grow from them. It is a little like selecting the best picture from a stack of proofs (or nowadays, which digital images to save and which ones to delete).

Every year, the day after Thanksgiving, we take our annual family photo. If we were to just take the picture with Barry and me, our three children and little grandson Skye, it probably would be easy. However, we like to get as many of our pets in the photo as possible. After all, they are an important part of the family.

In years past, we have included Rami's two horses, our multitude of dogs, and tried to include the five cats. However, the cats were the least cooperative so we gave up on them after trying five years in a row. The year 2013 was easy. Our golden retriever, Rosie, had nine puppies, so we all just held the puppies. We skipped all the other animals.

No one it seems, other than Barry and I, want this photo to be taken, so there are usually complaints. When my mother was alive, and Barry's mom was able to visit for Thanksgiving, we included them in the photo, but even they complained. Seems the complaining is just part of the experience. But once the photo is taken, everyone is happy to have one and even enjoys looking at the past ones.

So finally, when we have our animals all situated and the people in place, Barry sets the auto-timer and runs over to join the rest of us. Since we have a digital camera, we can see the results. Usually the first series of shots is terrible. The animals are all looking at the camera but we are all so busy with the animals that few of us are looking at the camera. We start again with the instruction to feel our love for one another. Out of the next bunch, there is typically one that is the charm. Perhaps not all of the animals and people are looking at the camera, but the love we have for one another is evident. So, in this way, we have our yearly photo.

Now, which is the photo we will remember as the true Vissell family photo? Will we remember the shots where one of us is frowning because an animal is not cooperating, or will we remember the one that shows our love for one another? This is the way it is in life and relationships. There are beautiful heartfelt moments, and moments when we are distracted from our hearts. Which do we choose to remember?

One Thanksgiving Day, when our children were small, Barry and I managed to take a lovely walk on the beach by ourselves. We hadn't had much time alone that past week, and so we enjoyed this rare opportunity. We talked about how grateful we were for one another and took time every so often to stop and have a leisurely kiss. We felt romantic and close.

Later that day, feeling tired, we were back in the kitchen preparing our vegetarian meal for our family and friends. Barry was sitting at the table chopping ingredients while I was cleaning up the kitchen. My eyes fell on a pot with burned oatmeal caked on the bottom. Since Barry had burned the pot, I insisted that he clean it himself. "I'll give the pot a good soaking," was his reply.

Three days into its soaking, I went over and started complaining about the pot. He glared back at me. It was a tense moment that took about five minutes to work through. Now, which moment shall I place in my memory bank for that Thanksgiving, the kisses and closeness on the beach or the burned oatmeal pot?

At the end of the second Harry Potter movie, *The Chamber of Secrets*, the great wizard Albus Dumbledore told

Harry that life is not only about how much talent we have. It's also the choices we make that make the difference. For that Thanksgiving, I prioritized the kisses and closeness over the burned oatmeal pot. I chose to remember love and, somewhere down the years, have this memory as a golden gem to remember.

A few days later, I entered the kitchen to see Barry scrubbing away at the pot. He looked up at me with a sheepish grin and said, "I guess it's soaked long enough." I went over and put my arms around him and told him how much I loved him.

Money and Loving a Man

YOU LOVE A MAN BY PARTICIPATING IN THE FINANCIAL SIDE OF THE RELATIONSHIP. In some families, it is the woman who handles all of the finances and, in other families, it is the woman who not only handles all of the finances but also earns all of the money. This was the case with Barry's parents. When Barry's father lost his job after a major auto accident, he became an artist, a career he loved but which earned him very little money. Barry's mother not only earned the money as a teacher, but she also did all the work of managing their finances.

However, I want to address the majority of families where the man handles the money and, in many cases, is the major money earner. This is particularly the case where there are young children in the family, and the mother is able to stay at home with them while the father works.

Even if your man earns all the money and pays all of the bills, it is still important to be aware of your family's finances and help in money decisions. He can feel lonely and isolated handling the money by himself. It can also be a controlling place where he is in a position of too much power. Either way, a woman loses her power in the relationship when she is unaware of the finances.

I have been in both situations until I stepped into equal participation in our finances. I know what both sides feel like, and neither side is comfortable. Being an equal partner is empowering for both the man and woman. It does not mean that the woman has to make as much money as the man, but it does mean that she participates in some way and is aware of their financial situation.

When we were first married, Barry had just started medical school. I worked as a nurse and supported both of us with my salary. I handled all of our finances for the first seven years of our marriage. At first, I was happy to do this and felt I was doing it for both of us and our future. Barry was unaware of the amount and the general flow of our money. He sometimes wanted to do things we could not afford. I had to say no, and it put our relationship in an unbalanced state. I became like the parent with the money, and he like a child asking for things we could not afford. This situation did not feel good to either of us.

Then we switched. I got pregnant and had our first child. Barry made more of the money and took over all of the finances. Now it was I who became totally unaware of our financial situation. In a way, I became like a child and he was the parent, telling me what we could or could not afford.

Each of the two situations was difficult for our relationship. After thirteen years and three children, I asked if I could be a full partner with him in the handling of our finances. Barry was greatly relieved as he wanted and needed the help. He is good with the details. Everything is carefully recorded in Quicken, something I can't ever see myself doing. But I have a much-needed overall sense and intuition about our financial situation. Because we are self-employed, our income is different every month, and I have a sense of how to deal with the lean months. I feel empowered as I am helping. Now we stand as equal partners. Neither one of us is the child asking the other for things we cannot afford. We both clearly understand our finances, and communicate before making any big decisions.

We once counseled a wealthy couple. Phillip made more money than most people. They lived in an extravagant home, drove expensive cars, had a big sailboat and sent their two daughters to an expensive private school. Each girl also had expensive ballet and music lessons each week. The budget was huge! Even though Phillip made a lot of money, he felt trapped and lonely, like he had to handle everything financially himself. Penny had no idea how much money they had. She bought expensive things for herself, the girls and their home. Phillip was afraid to say no to Penny so the spending grew and grew. Even though he made a lot of money, they were heavily in credit card debt.

With our help, Penny learned to love Phillip by becoming aware of their finances. Rather than just buying expensive things, she sat with him at the computer and *together* they made decisions. She even suggested ideas to help them get out of debt. She got a part-time job. Even though she did not earn much money, the money she did earn went toward her own private expenses like clothes, hair appointments and jewelry as well as her daughters' private ballet and music lessons. By her working and contributing as well as becoming a conscious and aware partner with her husband, they were soon able to get out of debt. Phillip no longer felt so trapped and lonely, and Penny felt empowered. Phillip was able to move out of the father role, handling all the money, and Penny was able to move out of the child role, spending all the money. Her move into helping her man was definitely a way of both loving him and herself.

When Barry and I started having children we rented a small farmhouse on a large piece of land for $270 per month. We didn't want money to be a big issue in our lives. We wanted to concentrate on being with our children as much as possible. We didn't own a credit card and had no debt for many years. We only bought things that we could pay for immediately. Our lives were extremely simple.

Then the 1989 earthquake destroyed the old farmhouse. A friend found us one of the only rental homes available after the earthquake ... for $1800 a month! It seemed like a waste of money to spend so much on rent, so we decided to follow a long-held dream, buy a piece of land and build a home that we could use as our center. We were able to buy sixteen acres that was right next to the destroyed house. This land was selling way below the market value as people were scared about another earthquake.

For the first time in our lives we were in debt. We got credit cards. We then built our home to be able to do our workshops there as well as raise our family of three children. When the home was finished and we finalized our mortgage, we were absolutely in shock to see how much money we owed. Our monthly payment actually scared us.

For the first time in our marriage we began fighting over money. We watched each other closely to see how the other could be more frugal. We criticized each other's spending. One day, after a particularly loud argument over money, we walked downstairs to find our three children huddled together. Mira, who was ten at the time, said, "Does this mean you're getting a divorce?"

We hugged the children, apologized, and told them we would always be together as a family. Rami, who was sixteen at the time, then said, "We're sick of hearing you fight over money. I'm taking Mira and John-Nuri, who was three, on a little adventure in the woods for a few hours. I want you to come up with a plan so you don't have to fight so much. And I want to hear your plan when I come back."

There's nothing like brutal honesty from your children to get you to quickly understand that change is in order. We sat together and thought of all the possible things we could do to stop this constant fighting. We knew we were afraid that, after building our dream home and center, we might lose it in a month or two. We needed help. From all of our spiritual work together we knew we were forgetting to ask for help from the highest source. We decided that our plan would be to put this financial challenge into higher hands. We would pray together every day and ask for help. And then we would do our best to meet this high mortgage payment.

Rami returned later that afternoon with Mira and John-Nuri in tow. We told her about our plan and she was satisfied. She did comment, "How come you didn't come up with that plan sooner?"

Every day since that day, we have asked for divine help with our finances. True, our money situation did not change overnight. There were still times that we wondered how we would come up with the money, but we kept on with our prayers and each month, by some miracle, just enough money was there. One month we were lacking $2,000 for the mortgage and it needed to be paid within a few days. We had no idea what we were going to do, but we prayed about it and tried to be in a state of peace. The next day, we received an unexpected check from our German publisher for $2,000. They never sold many books, but we did get a check every two or three years. This particular check showed up right on time!

Twenty-five years later, we are still saying those prayers and we have one and a half more years to go. We pray together every day, not just for financial matters, but also to be of service, praying for others and offering prayers of gratitude. Praying together has helped us tremendously with our financial situation as well as every other aspect of our relationship and lives. It gives us a feeling that we are not alone, but can rely on a greater help.

It is still a challenge to meet that mortgage payment each month. But it is a challenge we are meeting together and, through prayer, cooperation and sharing the concern, it has actually brought us closer together as a couple.

One of the Beatles, George Harrison, wrote shortly before he died about his regret at never struggling to come up with a mortgage payment. He missed the triumphant feeling of working hard to be able to pay for the roof over his head. Money came so easily to George and the other Beatles. He wished he could have had that basic feeling of accomplishment common to so many people.

It *is* a good feeling to meet our expenses each month and, by working together, it has brought us even more happiness.

Barry: Money is such a controversial topic in most relationships. What happens when the man you love is the one who earns more of the money? You love a man by appreciating his financial support, even if you are working just as hard in other ways, like with the children, or in a career that keeps you just as busy as he but returns less in monetary ways. Can you find frequent and different ways to acknowledge your partner's financial support of you? Hopefully, your man is appreciating your contribution just as much. If not, let him know that you need this. Most men deeply need to be acknowledged for how hard they work, and the money they bring home. You may not appreciate him for this, especially if you feel guilty for not earning as much money. Even if you work just as hard as he does, our culture assigns more value to the one who earns the most money. This ethic, absorbed into our cells since childhood, can be difficult to transcend. If you are taking care of the children at home, know that you are contributing just as much, if not more, to the family as he does.

What about the reverse? What if you are the main breadwinner? Because of cultural pressure, this can be damaging to his feelings of self-worth, even if he consciously made the decision for his lifestyle. Obviously, if he is lying around stoned or watching TV all day, he is clearly taking advantage of you. But if he is working just as hard as you in ways that don't bring in money, you love him by daily appreciating his work and effort as a contribution to the overall wellness of your family.

You hurt the relationship by wanting to be taken care of financially without wanting to contribute or even knowing anything about your family's financial picture. You are then like the ostrich hiding her head in the sand. Like Joyce said, you are then disempowering yourself and presenting yourself like a helpless and ignorant child to your partner. In *To Really Love a Woman*, we wrote about Ray, who made all the money and, in the name of protecting his wife, Kerry, kept their financial problems (and some bad financial decisions) hidden from her. This was, of course, a huge mistake on his part. Yet Kerry made the "ostrich" mistake.

She didn't want to know about their financial position. In this regard, she gave up her power to Ray, at least until she found out their home was in foreclosure!

You really love a man by taking an active interest in your combined financial picture, becoming an equal partner in managing your family finances. You have knowledge and skills he doesn't have. Each partner in a relationship brings a special strength to money matters. With the advent of the personal computer in the eighties, I soon became proficient with handling our family's finances. Joyce had no interest in learning Quicken, so I naturally took over paying the bills. But we made a mistake in this decision. I was trying to handle our financial situation all by myself, and Joyce was letting me do this. The result: we weren't doing well financially. I needed Joyce's input, and Joyce needed to be more involved. I was clearly better at the day-to-day managing, but Joyce was amazingly helpful with the overall vision and financial planning. When we worked together, combining our strengths, we naturally did much better financially.

In 2003 we refinanced our property yet again. We had the opportunity to significantly lower our interest rate, so we went ahead. Our friend and mortgage broker asked us if we wanted the traditional 30-year mortgage, or did we want to pay it off in 15 years? He showed us the huge amount of saved interest, and then the much higher monthly payment for the 15-year mortgage. I immediately said, "No way!"

Joyce put her hand on my arm. It was a comforting move, but somehow after all our years together, I knew what was coming. I didn't feel comforted.

"Barry," she gently began, "I know we can do this. Maybe it'll be a bit of a stretch in the beginning, but I trust that we'll be able to budget this into our lives. And just think, in 2018 we'll pay off our mortgage, and we'll only be 72 years old, rather than 87!"

I cringed at the thought of 15 years of intense struggle each month. I imagined sleepless nights, worrying about our finances, while most other people were enjoying a lazy retirement.

I looked at Joyce's smiling face, so trusting and innocent. What if, I thought, her beautiful trust wasn't grounded in reality? Or was this my fear expressing itself? Or my lack of trust?

A peaceful part of me knew Joyce was right. I had much to learn from her innocent faith. We signed for the 15-year mortgage.

The first year, I must admit, was challenging. The biggest challenge was getting hit with our property tax bill, for which we didn't budget. After that, Joyce again came to the rescue. We broke down our annual property tax and insurance totals into a monthly figure. Joyce had the brilliant idea to automatically transfer that amount into a separate account dedicated entirely to those two bills. I once again looked into her trusting eyes, but the words that came out were, "We can't afford that! Some months we won't have enough money in our account for the bank to transfer. We need to decide each month on our own."

And how did Joyce love me in that moment of fear and lack? "Barry," she gently said, again touching me lightly on my arm, "If we leave it up to us each month, we'll find excuses not to transfer the money. It's an act of trust in God's abundance to put it out of our own hands. You'll see. The money will be there each month."

Incredibly, it has! It's not that we're putting our heads in the sand. As the Sufis say, "Trust in Allah, but don't forget to tether your camel!" We are diligently working together as a couple, me especially on the day-to-day finances and Joyce especially on the long-range planning. But just as important are our daily prayers for spiritual help, and the trust we give to the Divine Banker, who is always watching out for our highest good. We have an innate trust that our desire to help others will actually be financed by the universe, and this brings us the most peace of all.

To Really Accept Who He Is

TO REALLY LOVE A MAN IS TO ACCEPT HIS ESSENCE. Of course there are things about him you would love to change, even things about him that drive you crazy. We're not asking you to lovingly accept the piles of dirty clothes strewn about, the excessive TV watching, the wet towel crumpled on the floor, or the unmade bed after he has slept in. These things may be annoying. More importantly, you may feel hurt by his not wanting to hear your feelings, the way he takes work-related stress out on you, or his lack of initiative in creating special time for the relationship.

Okay, it's time for me to confess. I've done all the above – and more. And has Joyce sweetly smiled and accepted these behaviors? I don't think so. When I annoy her, I hear about it fairly quickly. When I hurt her, though, I hear about it immediately. I feel loved by her even when she is annoyed by my behavior. I feel accepted by her even when she is hurt by the things I say or do. My soul, who I am at the deepest level, my essence, feels loved and accepted, even when some of my actions or inactions are not loved or accepted.

I'm a bit more compulsive than Joyce with my dental care. Okay, I'm a lot more compulsive. It doesn't work for me to use the Sonicare toothbrush, with its loud whine, standing next to her in the bathroom. And when it comes time for me to rinse with mouthwash, my extra thoroughness just about drives her crazy if I'm anywhere close to her. She wonders why I can't quietly swish. Why does it have to sound like a washing machine on heavy-duty cycle? She expresses her annoyance when I forget and do these things too close to her. Still, I feel Joyce's clear differentiation between my soul and my actions.

Then there's loving behavior modification. When Joyce comes upstairs and sees that I am using the Sonicare or "swishing" my mouthwash in the bedroom, away from her, she makes it a point to acknowledge this as a loving act toward her. The result: it reinforces my change of behavior.

One of our dogs, Emma, had somehow developed the habit of relieving herself exactly in the middle of the trail, road, or wherever we happened to be walking. Our other dogs were more respectful, making their deposits off the road or trail. The consequences of Emma's behavior were obvious, especially if we were walking in the dark or not paying close attention to each step. Rarely, we observed her squatting off to the side, and seized the opportunity to lavish praise upon her. It's called effective dog training, but it works just as well with humans.

You might have noticed by now that complaining or nagging just doesn't work. Pay close attention, be extra vigilant for good behaviors, and praise him enthusiastically in the moment. Don't wait till later. By the time Emma took two steps away from her off-trail deposit, it was too late to praise her effectively as a training tool. While a man usually has somewhat longer short-term memory than a dog, acknowledging good behaviors right in the moment still works best.

Most importantly, Joyce lets me know how happy she is to be with me, that she loves the whole package of me. She sometimes tells me, if I were gone, how much she would miss everything about me, even the smelly gas rising out of the covers in the middle of the night.

She may not accept certain of my behaviors, but she accepts the ways I am different from her. She understands that if I were more like her I wouldn't challenge her to grow as much. She loves my adventurous spirit that sometimes has to force her out of her comfort zone. While she would be perfectly content going for an hour-long day-hike, I motivate her to accompany me on overnight backpacking or river trips.

She loves how I rarely get stuck in my feelings. If something painful has happened that affects us both, Joyce will process it in her feelings for a long time. Perhaps, during a walk together, she will need the first thirty minutes to talk with me about the issue. And during this time she really appreciates my listening, as well as my help and insights. Then we may walk for five or ten minutes in silence. During this time she continues to go over her feelings, while I am busy noticing the trees, the sun, the path we are on, what the dogs are up to, or an owl that has just silently flown from a tree. Joyce is amazed that I have not even given one passing thought to the issue. She loves and accepts how different I am from her.

On occasion, I embarrass my precious beloved with my gregariousness. Once, on a hike with Joyce in Norway in the fall, we came upon a patch of rose hips tastier and more succulent than any I had ever sampled in this country. Usually rose hips are quite tart. I simply got excited. At that moment, a young woman was jogging past us. Without thinking, I started enthusiastically pointing out the patch of rose hips to her. Her eyes flashed alarm and fear as if she were in the presence of a crazy man, and she turned her face away from me and quickened her pace as she passed us. Even though Joyce was embarrassed in that moment, she loves and accepts the innocent enthusiasm that is at the root of my actions.

Not long ago, we were invited to be visiting teachers for a week at Esalen Institute on the Big Sur coast of California. Our job involved working with the staff and volunteers each evening. During dinner in the large dining room before our first evening's meeting, I stood up, started tapping a glass with a spoon to get everyone to be quiet, and announced our class while Joyce shrank lower in her seat. Joyce gets embarrassed by my chutzpah, the way I can take risks where I might look like a fool. Okay, quite often I do look like a fool. At the same time, she appreciates that this quality is part of who I am. She appreciates that I care little about what people think of me.

Inner Practice

> Take some time to separate his actions from who he is. See who he really is, the being behind the doing. What are the unique qualities of his soul? You may not accept some behaviors, but spend this time accepting who he really is.

You Love Him by Knowing You Are Equals

A POWERFUL WAY TO LOVE A MAN IS TO SEE THE EQUALITY IN BOTH OF YOU. Many women feel that, because they read more spiritual books, they are more spiritual, or because they read more self-help books and go to seminars, they are more advanced than their man. To really love your man, see the equality of the beauty, spirituality and growth that is present in him in a different way than in you.

At a recent couples retreat, a man started talking about how much further ahead his wife was: "She reads a lot of self-help books, goes to workshops, meditates, and does yoga. I only provide for the family and, in my free time, spend as much time with my family as I possibly can." Then he placed one hand higher than the other and sadly said, "She is up here and I am down here, and I don't think I can ever catch up with her."

Barry and I looked over at his wife who also sadly agreed with all he said. This perception, we knew, was going to keep them from feeling totally connected. And yet, looking at this couple, we couldn't help but notice the equality of love in both of them. I told them a story about myself that happened in 1980:

Barry and I lived a quiet life with our four-year-old daughter, Rami, in the woods and hills outside of Santa Cruz, California. We had a small rented house with hundreds of acres of land to explore. Except for an occasional trip into town for groceries, we saw almost no one. Our days were mostly filled with caring for and playing with our small daughter. While one of us was watching Rami, the other would meditate, do yoga or read spiritual books. Barry also worked one or two days a week at a clinic as a doctor to support our simple lifestyle. My spiritual practice was disciplined. I meditated long hours and seriously read various spiritual books. Barry started out that way, but gradually other things took more and more of his attention. He learned how to do many of the repairs on our 1970 Volkswagen bus, he built trails to hike on, he did woodworking, and studied maps and trail books for adventures to be had someday. While my spiritual practice grew and grew, Barry devoted less and less time to that pursuit. I began to feel that I was better than Barry, even, I hate to admit, spiritually superior to him. The more I felt superior, the greater the distance grew between us.

Right at this time, I needed to take a continuing education class to keep my nursing license, so I chose a weekend workshop on inner healing away from home. As soon as I signed up for the workshop, a strong intuitive feeling came over me that I would meet a new man and fall in love with him. This thought both intrigued and scared me. I hadn't been interested in anyone else since I met Barry in 1964.

The day of the workshop arrived. I kissed and said good-bye to Barry and our darling daughter for three days, then traveled 50 miles south to attend the workshop. The whole time I was driving, I was aware of my unsettling feeling that I would be meeting and falling in love with a new man. I also felt some guilt that I didn't tell Barry about this strange premonition.

I entered the workshop room with trepidation and saw there were only a few men in a roomful of women, and these men were much older than I was. I immediately thought, "Wow, my intuition was really wrong this time."

That taken care of, I settled into the course. The instructor had us choose one area in our lives that needed healing. I chose this feeling of superiority over Barry. Throughout the next three days he led us in meditations in which we saw the healing taking place. With each meditation, I concentrated on the ways that Barry really was spiritual. As I did this, I realized that spirituality isn't about how much a person does. It is more about their heart or essence. As the weekend progressed, I realized that I was seeing Barry in a new light.

Not being able to stand being apart from him, I called and asked him to join me for the last afternoon of the workshop. Barry found a babysitter and hitchhiked down to be with me.

When I saw him, I felt like I was seeing the man of my dreams. I ran into his waiting arms. The older nurses witnessing this scene asked if we were newly in love. I actually did feel newly in love with the most wonderful, spiritual man.

Outwardly, Barry hadn't changed a drop. He had just been spending ordinary days with Rami, something he often did. But I saw him in a new way, and that made all the difference. My premonition was right! I truly had fallen in love with a new man.

Nine years later, two more children, three books written, and having a busy complicated lifestyle, the 1989 Loma Prieta earthquake totally destroyed that wonderful rented house. We were all inside and narrowly escaped with our lives. Immediately after the earthquake, we somehow made our way out of the mess that used to be our home. I carried our five-month-old John-Nuri, while Rami and our seven-year-old daughter, Mira, were helped out by Barry. I felt in shock and just stood silently out in the street, while Mira asked me if we had just died and gone to heaven. Barry, to my complete surprise, put his arms around us and began thanking God for sparing our lives and allowing us all to make it out safely. Through my shock and confusion, I looked at him and marveled at his immediate and enthusiastic spiritual response to our situation. I also wondered how I could have ever felt superior to him in this regard.

Today, I continue to devote more of my free time to my spiritual practices than Barry does. But if I ever think that perhaps I am ahead of him in this regard, I have only to picture him holding his family and thanking God, while our home and possessions were all destroyed. Spirituality is more about our hearts, the way we live our lives, the way we care about others and ourselves, than it is about the amount of time we spend with books or practices.

To Really Love the Man Within

JOYCE AND I BOTH FEEL THAT OUR SOULS, the essential part of us, are both feminine and masculine. The highest marriage, the most spiritual joining, takes place within ourselves, not with an outer partner. True, the relationship we have with another person can mirror this inner relationship, and help point the way to the real joining within us. Yet it is seductively easy to get lost in the outer relationship and perhaps completely miss the most important relationship. The illusion of relationship is that it only takes place outside of you. The truth about relationship is that it mostly takes place within you.

How much you love your inner man determines how much you love your outer man. If you refuse to love your inner maleness, you will try in vain to really love the man in your life. If you right now are feeling resistant to this concept, this chapter may be the most important chapter in this book.

Projection is an often subtle force in relationships. The love we need from a man is the love we have within us already. It's just easier to see, or want, that love from our male partner.

Does that mean we don't need the outer man, that we only have to receive what we need from our inner man? Some might then say, "Why bother with outer relationships at all? It's just a distraction from the most important work within. I can join a monastic order or just stay at home and meditate on my inner man." Certainly, this is always an option, but we say that the path of conscious relationship with a male partner can powerfully teach you about your inner man. Loving the man in your life can provide the fastest path to loving your inner man. Accepting the maleness you see and feel in your partner is a powerful way to accept your inner maleness.

Positive Projections Can Also Hurt

Barry and I accept that there are negative projections, qualities we don't like in our man that are reflections of qualities we don't like in ourselves. One example could be our partner's expression of anger, and our judgment that we have less anger than him. Perhaps we hold back our own expression of anger, but we have just as much anger inside. It's just easier to see his problem with anger than our own.

However, positive projections, the goodness in ourselves that we can only see in our man, can just as much stand in the way of relationship growth. When we see more beauty or strength in our man than we do in ourselves, we do not feel equal to him. We put him onto a pedestal, higher than ourselves and, thus, cannot have closeness. When we understand relationship as a mirror, we can realize the beauty we have projected onto him is also within ourselves. Such a realization can restore equality to the relationship, and spiritual balance within ourselves.

An example of an unhealthy positive projection took place in our own early relationship. In 1972, when Barry was a psychiatry resident, I worked in the department of child psychiatry at the University of Oregon Medical Center. Since the adult and child psychiatry departments were near each other, I always knew where Barry was. Whenever he was leading a group, it was easy for me to slip into the observation room to watch him through the window that was a mirror to him and the group. Usually, Barry's teachers and fellow residents were also in the little room for the purpose of critiquing his effectiveness with the group. I ignored their comments and concentrated all my attention upon Barry. More than simply being effective, I thought he was brilliant and compassionate.

One day, one of the psychiatrists, and also a friend of both of ours, noticed my joy-filled observation. She leaned close to me and whispered, "You could do just as good a job as Barry is doing right now."

I quickly responded, "Oh no, no. He has the gift. I could never do anything like that."

She smiled and said, "Look inside yourself."

These last words impacted me deeply. I had always assumed Barry was better than me when it came to leading groups. I also felt he had better social skills. He was more outgoing and spoke freely with everyone. It seemed that people liked him more than me.

These positive projections were standing in the way of my feeling my own abilities and strengths. Gradually, the words of the psychiatrist began to sink in. All this time, I thought I was looking *through* the mirror of the observation room when, in fact, I was looking *into* a mirror. I realized a powerful truth: *what we see in another, we already have in ourselves*. It wasn't wrong to see so much greatness in Barry. It was wrong to not see the greatness in myself. Seeing Barry as having something I didn't have was putting him on a pedestal above me and, therefore, preventing us from true closeness.

In the years that followed, with the help of friends and teachers, I grew in awareness of my own beauty and lovability. Rather than ceasing to see and appreciate the gifts of my beloved husband, because of my acceptance of my own gifts, I could see his even more clearly. Through reclaiming what I saw in the mirror of my relationship, I grew in self-acceptance and self-confidence and allowed a deeper closeness in our relationship.

Barry and I now enjoy leading groups together, which brings a deep fulfillment to both of us. Barry's style is often different than my style, but the group needs the combination of both our styles. Recognizing my own strengths has allowed my leadership to be rewarding, purposeful and fun.

Practice: Loving your Inner Man

Sit or stand in front of a mirror. Look deeply into your own eyes. This takes time and practice. Most people find it difficult to do this. You might be tempted to give up after a brief try, but please don't. This simple practice can change your whole life.

Breathe deeply and slowly. Allow each conscious breath to take you deeper into your eyes, the windows of your soul, which is both feminine and masculine.

Concentrate on seeing your inner man. There are qualities you attribute to men that you don't attribute to yourself. Find out what they are by looking deeply at your inner maleness.

They may be positive qualities like strength, patience, assuredness, wisdom, competence, coordination, physical ability, protection, playfulness, humor, or one-pointed focus. Your work is to see and accept all these "masculine" qualities in yourself. This will allow you to really love a man.

They may be negative qualities like immaturity, rigidity, emotional incompetence, competitiveness, aggression, seriousness, distractibility, or impulsivity. Yes, these too are also within you. You really love a man by accepting these qualities in you, rather than only projecting them onto him.

If you want to be a better lover, do not avoid the mirror. Use it more than only to brush your hair, floss your teeth, put on your makeup, or criticize your latest wrinkles. The mirror is a powerful tool for loving the man in your life by loving the man within you.

To Know the God in Your Man

TO REALLY LOVE A MAN IS TO KNOW THE DIVINE, eternal being shining out from within him. It's not enough to know his outer beauty, no matter how captivated you are by it. If you take the time to really look into his eyes, the windows of the soul, you will see a god, a vast, ageless, beautiful expression of the divine masculine.

What you most love about him is his god-self, the highest truth of his being. When he looks really good, you are getting a glimpse of who he really is. When he looks at you with loving eyes, you are feeling loved by God through him. When he touches you with love, can you feel how much more it is than a touch by a person?

Please understand, this is something *you* do, a way *you* love him. It doesn't work to just wait for him to manifest his divine self. This is part of your spiritual work on the relationship.

There's a great word and gesture in the Hindu religion: Namaste (Nah'-mah-stay). It is often said as a greeting with hands palm-to-palm against your chest at the level of your heart. It has been loosely translated as "I honor the God/Goddess within you." This greeting acknowledges that we are all so much more than we seem.

You most deeply love your man by acknowledging the greatness of his inner self. That is the real opportunity of relationship. It doesn't matter what he does or doesn't do, whether he prays, meditates, or does any spiritual practice. He, like you, has greatness of soul, sometimes hidden by his body or personality. If you look for it, you will see it. If you ignore his divine self, it will remain hidden to you.

Joyce loves me the most by seeing and knowing who I really am, especially when I don't. She loves my spiritual nature, the deepest part of me. I feel she has always seen my divine self, and most of the time has compassion when I live in the smaller part of me. She has learned not to judge my spirituality based on what I do, but she knows my spirituality as who I am.

Joyce loves me by continuing our relationship when we're not together. I stay in her thoughts and feelings. Sometimes, it's easier for her to feel my Higher Self when she's not distracted by my physical self. We call this "practicing the presence of each other." She feels my true presence, the part of me she loves the most. It's a meditation for Joyce, but one she can do throughout the day, even when she's active. I know when she has been feeling my Higher Self because of the unique way she looks at me.

I feel loved by my wife because of what she saw inside me when we were first dating. She was the first and only person in my life that truly looked into my heart and saw my potential as a human being, a husband and a father. When we first met, I did not feel worthy of someone so wonderful and beautiful. I could not even look into her eyes. She taught me how to be loved, feel important, and leave all my fragile insecurities behind. She did this by focusing on all my positive traits and not on the negative. My wife really wanted to have children and I remember telling her early on that I did not think I could have children. Her reaction was, "That's OK, I still love you and want to spend the rest of my life with you." Well, it turns out I was wrong and we had three children of our own, but her reaction to this situation made me feel like I was the most important person in her life and made me feel really loved, and it has lasted for 48 wonderful years. –Ed Stamas, Colrain, MA

Joyce: When I was a child I had several mystical experiences that involved Jesus. He became my best friend, my comforter, my guide and a source of steady love. My love for Jesus was simple, non-religious, non-judgmental, just the pure love of a child. When I became confirmed in our church and knelt before the altar, I felt a distinct presence of Jesus placing his hand on my head. I felt safe in my devotions to Jesus.

When I grew into a young adult, I found myself in several churches where Jesus was portrayed as a scary kind of judge who was watching out if I sinned and was grading my performance. Since none of us are perfect, I felt that most of the time I was probably failing. I also experienced people confronting me in a judgmental way and asking if I was "saved." If I tried to explain that I felt close to Jesus since childhood, they usually responded by saying it wasn't good enough and I wasn't actually saved. I had enough of these experiences to close my heart and mind, and I eventually put Jesus in a distant, hidden place within me. Sadly, I came to think that maybe those wonderful experiences of my childhood were just fantasy.

Years later, I was playing with three-year-old Rami in our living room. It was evening and we were having so much fun together. Barry was working at a hospital for a thirteen-hour shift as a general physician. While Rami and I were playing happily, a song came on from an old cassette I had forgotten about. Something about the words of the song brought me right back to the beautiful, uncomplicated feelings I had about Jesus as a child. I looked over at Rami and she was so sweet and innocent, just like I had been at the time of those mystical experiences. In that moment I yearned with all my heart to experience Jesus again in such a pure and beautiful way. I wanted a vision of Him to help me to know that my childhood experiences were real. Tears came to my eyes.

Rami noticed my tears and asked what was wrong. I told her in simple language that she could understand. She took my hand and said, "Mama, let's ask God to send a vision of Jesus to you tonight." Then she bowed her head and prayed for that gift. We continued our play until it was time for her to go to bed. As I settled into sleep, I remembered her simple prayer said in such faith. I closed my eyes and asked God to send me a vision of Jesus. At the time I remember feeling that I needed this more than anything else.

Barry usually came home around midnight after his marathon of seeing patients. I had rules concerning his return to our home. I did not want Barry to wake me up, as I got up early with Rami. I did not want him coming into our bedroom without taking a shower first. Being sensitive, I could feel the energy of so many patients all around him. He would take a shower and then quietly come to bed. This happened over and over again, week after week.

To help him stay awake, Barry usually listened to his rock and roll cassettes during the hour ride back to our home. But this particular night, he reached into his pile of tapes and put one up in front of his face. It was "The Messiah," by Handel. Rather than put it back and find a rock and roll tape, he chose to listen to this spiritual music during the ride home. He had never done that before, since the slowness of the songs would have normally put him to sleep, and he needed all the energy he could get after such an intense day.

When he arrived home, he also ignored my rule of always taking a shower before entering our bedroom. He immediately came into our bedroom and kneeled down close to me just to watch me sleep. He felt inspired.

Barry's presence near me brought me out of a deep sleep. I opened my eyes and there before me was the vision of Jesus I had prayed for. And then I heard these words inside of me: "Love the beautiful feeling of Jesus which resides within Barry and comes through his heart." I reached up and hugged Barry as he lovingly tried to explain, "I know the rules, but for some reason I was so strongly guided to come right in to be with you like this."

That experience has had a powerful impact upon my heart. Through loving Barry, I am also allowing my love for God and Jesus to come forth. I recalled the work of Mother Teresa in which she sees the Christ in each dying person that she tenderly cares for and loves.

I wish I could say that I love Barry with that kind of deep devotion all of the time. The truth is I don't, though I wish I could. But there are moments in every week when I look at him and experience the presence of God. It only takes a few seconds like that to change the energy between us. Perhaps it is a look or a feeling of love passing between us that allows us to experience the higher self of each. And these moments of pure love shine like a beautiful light over us as we go about our busy days. However brief these moments of seeing the God in Barry, it is the highest gift of love that I can give him.

Inner Practice: Communing with His God Self

> In the quiet of meditative reflection, after taking some deep quieting breaths, acknowledge you are more than your body, mind, feelings, and experiences. Give yourself a precious moment to accept your divinity, the being of light that you really are. Visualize and/or feel yourself as a being of light, with this light radiating from every part of you. Even physicists are discovering that the physical world is not so physical at all. Everything is made of light.
>
> If you skip this step, how can you expect to see the god in him? If you can accept, even a little bit, your own godhood, your own inherent light, the next part of the practice will flow naturally.
>
> Now picture the man you love. Bring him face to face with you so you can clearly see his eyes. Even just doing this will often allow you to see his eternal being.
>
> Next, imagine a light filling and surrounding his face. Even a glimpse of this light is enough to illumine his god self. Trust that this visualization is one of the highest ways to love yourself *and* him.

Outer Practice: Seeing His God Self

Invite your partner to sit facing you. Make a date or set a time to do this practice. Let him know you want to do this practice. If he hasn't read this little chapter and practice, let him read it or read it to him.

Start with eyes closed. Acknowledge a higher power within you ... your eternal, spiritual, divine self.

When you're both ready, open your eyes and gaze into each other's eyes. This is not a staring contest! There's a way to practice "soft" eye contact by focusing on your breath and relaxing your abdomen. If you focus too much attention on what you see, and not enough on your breath and relaxing, you may abandon yourself in a way. The secret is to stay with your own goddess self, which will allow you to behold his god self.

You or your partner may not feel comfortable looking so deeply into one another's eyes. It takes practice, so don't be discouraged if one of you needs to stop before the other is ready. Also, don't be disappointed if his face seems to go through a se-

> ries of changes, even faces that aren't familiar. This may be part of the process of the journey from the physical to the spiritual.
>
> It can help to close your eyes for a while to regroup, then begin again. Each time you do this practice, you will become more and more comfortable with longer periods of eye contact. The goal is not to see how long you can look into one another's eyes. It's not a marathon! The goal is to catch a glimpse of the radiant, exquisitely beautiful eternal face of your beloved. Even a few seconds of seeing the light within him is enough to bring your relationship to a higher love.

The great poet, Rumi, says, "There are a thousand ways to kneel and kiss the ground." We sincerely hope you can also know there are a thousand ways (and more) to love a man. May what we have written in this book inspire you to find even more ways.

Barry, you are the most wonderful life-partner. You are truly a great soul, and I feel privileged and honored to be your wife. I feel so grateful every day for the deep and profound love that we share.

Just by being in this world, you bring so much light, and are a shining example of a man living from his heart. I love your humility and deep spiritual nature. I also think you are delightfully funny.

My wish and hope for both of us is that we can live in health and service to God for many years to come, and that this beautiful love can only grow. I love you forever,

Joyce Vissell, May 27, 2004

About the Authors

The Vissells' books have been translated into five languages. They lecture and lead about 20 workshops per year internationally to audiences who welcome their warm, relaxed and yet profound wisdom. Joyce and Barry have written a monthly column for over 30 years, "New Dimensions of Relationship," which they email for free to anyone.

These articles also appear in about 80 print publications internationally, and countless e-zines, websites (including their own), and blogs.

Ram Dass describes Joyce and Barry Vissell "as a couple who live the yoga of love and devotion." Marianne Williamson says, "I can't think of anything more important to the healing of our society than a connection between spirituality, relationship and parenthood. Bravo to the Vissells for helping us find the way."

Barry and Joyce are two people deeply in love since 1964, who have raised three children and "walk their talk." They are the authors of *The Shared Heart, Models of Love, Risk To Be Healed, The Heart's Wisdom, Meant To Be,* and *A Mother's Final Gift*. A story from *Meant To Be* was made into a Sunday Night NBC Movie, *"It Must Be Love,"* starring real-life couple, Ted Danson and Mary Steenburgen.

The Vissells, since 1983, are the founders and directors of the Shared Heart Foundation, a non-profit organization dedicated to changing the world one heart at a time (SharedHeart.org).

Joyce and Barry live at their retreat center and home near Santa Cruz, California, where they counsel individuals and couples, and lead retreats and trainings when they're not travelling.

Go to **SharedHeart.org** to sign up for their **free heartletter**, to read past articles on many aspects of personal growth and relationship, to see their event or workshop schedule, or to contact Barry or Joyce.

ALSO BY THE VISSELLS

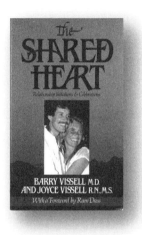

THE SHARED HEART
Relationship Initiations and Celebrations
ISBN 0-9612720-0-7, 186 pages,
©1984, Ramira Publishing, $9.95

The Shared Heart was one of the first books to bridge the chasm between following a spiritual path and having a deeply committed love relationship. As the book says, "Loving one other person teaches you how to love all people."

"The Shared Heart is full of beauty and compassion, richness and clarity. Barry and Joyce plough through the hard and soft spaces of the journey with great inner strength and deep respect for reflective inner tuning." —**Ram Dass**

"From the perspectives of romance, marriage, making love, parenting, careers, spiritual initiation, and loss of a loved one, this remarkable couple exhibits insight, acceptance and transcendence, at the same time offering specific tools for the transformational process of love."
—**Yoga Journal**

MODELS OF LOVE
The Parent-Child Journey
ISBN 0-9612720-1-5, 320 pages,
©1986, Ramira Publishing, $12.95

Contributors include Jack Kornfield, Eileen Caddy, Leo Buscaglia, Jerry Jampolsky, Joan Hodgson, Jeannine Parvati Baker and others.

"Our children need not fall asleep to the beauty of their heavenly state for twenty, thirty, or more years, at which time breaking the habit of material thought is very difficult. We can help them begin the awakening process from the day they are conceived, so that the bridge of consciousness between the two worlds is continually strengthened."

"This is a book we whole-heartedly recommend to first-time parents, to grandparents, and to everyone in between."
—**Mothering Magazine**

"Models of Love is more than a parenting book. It will bless your whole life!" —**John Bradshaw**

"This book is full of miraculous incidents and sacred moments of loving connection that will bring tears to your eyes."
—**Whole Life Magazine**

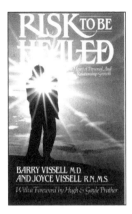

RISK TO BE HEALED
The Heart of Personal and Relationship Growth
ISBN 0-9612720-2-3, 192 pages, ©1989, Ramira Publishing, $9.95

Not infrequently, we receive an email or a letter with the words, "Your book has changed my life." Almost without exception, the writer is referring to *Risk to Be Healed*.

"In this book, Joyce & Barry offer the priceless gift of their own experience with relationship, commitment, vulnerability, and loss, along with the profound guide to healing that comes from the core of their being and blesses us with gentle wisdom."
—**Gayle & Hugh Prather**

The Vissells, in their uniquely captivating and personally revealing way, extend another written offering to the world. *Risk to be Healed* is filled with stories from their own continuing growth, as well as the healing risks individuals and couples have taken in their counseling sessions and workshops. The book begins with the profound experience of Anjel's death in utero and her subsequent birth into the lives of the authors. Subject matter includes: risk-taking in relationship, the way of intimacy, the power of right livelihood, understanding pain, healing relationships with those who have passed on, addictions, appreciation, vulnerability, and simplifying our lives.

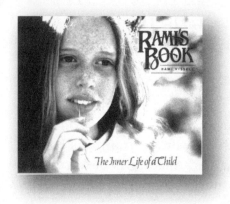

RAMI'S BOOK
The Inner Life of a Child

by Rami Vissell
ISBN 0-9612720-4-X, hardcover, 56 pages, full-color illustrated, ©1989, Ramira Publishing, $13.95

"We have been taught for a long time that the entrance to God's presence is through the eyes of a child. Rami flings wide that delicious door of perception."
—**Rev. Stan Hampson, Past President, Association of Unity Churches**

"My hope is that all adults as well as children may benefit by the understanding and love that Rami shares in this delightful book."
—**Ken Keyes**

"Rami's book is a gift from an angel. The innocent beauty filling these pages brings me tears of joy. I wish children of all ages would read this book." —**Alan Cohen**

"Of all the books I've reviewed, this one went right to my heart and made me cry quite wonderfully. Truly an angelic and marvelous work, and a gift to the child still within me. I put it on display with a sign: 'very, very highly recommended. 4 stars on the goose bump chart!'."
—**Richard Rodgers, manager, The Grateful Heart Bookstore.**

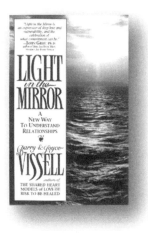

LIGHT IN THE MIRROR
A New Way to Understand Relationships
ISBN: 0-9612720-5-8, ©1995, Ramira Publishing, $13.95

"*Light in the Mirror is an expression of deep love and vulnerability, and the celebration of what commitment can be.*" —**John Gray, PhD**, author of *Men Are From Mars, Women Are From Venus.*

"*In* Light in the Mirror, *Joyce and Barry Vissell share with deep tenderness and vulnerability the valleys and peaks of their relationship. They go on to share 'practical spirituality,' suggestions that will be most helpful to everyone finding their way home to the heart.*"
—**Gerald Jampolsky, MD** and **Diane Cirincione**, authors of *Love is the Answer* and *Change Your Mind, Change Your Life.*

"*We have always benefited from the gentle wisdom of the Vissells.* Light in the Mirror *is one of the rare voices for sanity in the field of relationships.*" —**Gayle and Hugh Prather**, authors of *Notes to Myself* and *I Will Never Leave You.*

"*If you had but one book to choose to renew your relationship, this should be the one.*" —**Small Press Magazine**

"*Light in the Mirror is a must for anyone who yearns for better connection and more joy in their intimate relationships.*"
—**Napra Review**

MEANT TO BE
Miraculous True Stories To Inspire A Lifetime Of Love
ISBN 1-57324-161-X, ©2000, Conari Press, $14.95

"The true miracle of these stories is that they open your heart to your own miracle, for the miracle of love is within you too, and your story can be as magical as these. That is the healing message on Meant to Be, that is its wonder." – **Neale Donald Walsch**, author of *Conversations with God*

"Few books make me cry, but this one did, many times. The best collection of heart-full stories that I have ever read!" – **Mary Jane Ryan**, author of *Random Acts of Kindness*

"The Vissells, who themselves were brought together by Love and whose life work has been guided by Love, now bring us deeply moving (and some very entertaining) true accounts of Love's presence in the lives of other couples. Meant To Be says to us all, 'Relax. There are no chance encounters.'"
—**Hugh Prather**, author of *Notes to Myself*

A MOTHER'S FINAL GIFT
How One Woman's Courageous Dying Transformed Her Family
ISBN-13: 978-0-9612720-3-6, ©2011, Ramira Publishing, $14.95 US

"As we gave my mother her final gift on honoring her dying process, she gave us her final gift of opening a window into eternity and allowing us to have a peek."

A Mother's Final Gift is the story of one courageous woman – Louise Viola Swanson Wollenberg – and of her tremendous love of life and family, and her faith and resolve. But it is also the story of her equally courageous family who, in the process of rising to the occasion and carrying out Louise's long-held final wishes, not only overcame so many stigmas about the process of death but, at the same time, rediscovered what it means to celebrate life itself. This book not only touches the heart in a very powerful, poignant, and joyful way, but reading it was life-changing for me. In writing this book, Joyce and Barry Vissell, and their children, mentor us through an experience that many of us were afraid to even think about it. Louise looked at death as her greatest adventure. So should we all. The title of this book is indeed A Mother's Final Gift but, in truth, this story is an exceptional gift to every person who will read it. **– George Daugherty**, Emmy Award-winning producer, director, and conductor